CHARACTER COUNTS

WHO'S COUNTING YOURS?

ROD HANDLEY

CHARACTER COUNTS— WHO'S COUNTING YOURS?

Library of Congress Cataloging-in-Publication Data

ISBN 1-887002-00-6
Handley, Rod
Rod Handley

CHARACTER COUNTS—WHO'S COUNTING YOURS? / Rod Handley
Published by Cross Training Publishing, Grand Island, Nebraska 68803

Distributed in the United States and Canada by Cross Training Publishing

Cover Illustration: Jeff Sharpton
Printed in the United States of America

Contents

For additional books and resources available
through Cross Training Publishing contact us at:

Cross Training Publishing
P.O. Box 1541
Grand Island, NE 68802
(308) 384-5762

Foreword

Rod Handley has addressed the area of personal accountability in a very candid and practical manner. He writes as though he is talking with you one on one. He gives the basic principles of developing an accountability relationship and the disciplines of living a genuine Christian life.

Over the past several years, accountability partners have helped and encouraged me in many ways. Each of them has played a part in my own journey to serve and love the Lord Jesus Christ.

The tough questions that John Wesley used almost 300 years ago and the accountability model suggested by Rod works. People who lead lives of integrity will embrace accountability because they hide nothing from the Lord and people. Unfortunately, there are people lacking character in the world today; people leading lives of "secret" sin and worldly pleasures, with no one asking tough, hard questions directed at the very soul. It is a true blessing to look your partners in the eye after making a covenant of accountability.

This is a practical tool to make a real impact in the lives of men and women who desire to be people of integrity. With accountability you will confront areas of your life which need to be addressed. You will not regret making a commitment to accountability.

Dal Shealy
President, Fellowship of Christian Athletes

INTRODUCTION AND ACKNOWLEDGMENTS

Every day we are faced with decisions. Each decision made either enhances or damages our character. Character also deals with the issues pertaining to making and keeping your commitments. Fellowship of Christian Athletes staff member Larry Medcalfe formed an accountability group several years ago which he described as an "ABC Group." ABC stood for "Accountability Builds Character." If you want to take a huge step in building your character, then this book is for you.

"Character Counts—Who's Counting Yours?" has been an eighteen month project. During that time, there have been so many lessons I have learned. This is a concise look at the issue of accountability. It is the buzz word of the 1990's, yet when it really gets down to the specifics, very few know how to implement it into daily life. Here is my attempt to bring it into one book.

You will not find the word "accountability" in the Bible, yet the principles are found throughout. Accountability is asking someone to help enhance your relationship with Jesus Christ. As you place your trust in Christ, He is the only one who can meet your needs. He has to be the first one you turn to for instruction and guidance. Your accountability partners play an important, secondary role in your spiritual growth and maturity. One person described being in an accountability group as a "buried treasure" and that many treasures are available to each one of us if we would allow people to ask difficult questions.

"Character Counts—Who's Counting Yours?" is broken into two sections. The first section defines accountability by breaking down the who, what, where, when and why issues. The second section breaks down the ten questions which our group answers each week. Each chapter ends with a special story, lesson or poem which ties back to the chapter topic. Ideally, you will get through this book in approximately two hours and have a solid basis for beginning your own group and with tools to put it together.

Because the chapters could be one or several volumes in and of themselves, I have given you basic information to help you get started. If you want to get more detailed on the areas mentioned in Chapters 8-17, I encourage you to seek out your local church or Christian book store for resources to aid you.

This book should help meet the needs of both males and females, young and old, plus cross cultural and denominational lines. Though it is not intended to be all things to all people, you can refer to the scripture references and various suggestions to help guide you in your daily life.

A special thanks to my accountability group for their input to the project along the way. Also, my wife, Janna, was so supportive of this effort during the entire time and also provided her insight and prayers. I am also thankful for my editor, Don Hilkemeier, who not only provided the final touches but also is a wonderful friend and co-laborer in the gospel. George Toles was responsible for providing the title of this book, along with some key editorial comments and much encouragement along the way. I also want to thank my publisher, Gordon Thiessen for agreeing to do this book—sight unseen. What a wonderful blessing to have someone catch a vision with you even when the dream is still in the infancy stages.

Many other people along the way gave me encouragement and information. People like Chuck Snyder, Chip Lambert, Scott Kessler, Deb Shepley, Becky Bowman, Dan Dolquist, Jake Combs, Craig Hamilton, Kathy Cosgrove and numerous FCA staff members and volunteers across the country were helpful in many ways. All in all, it was a true team effort and to God be the glory! My prayer from the beginning has been from John 3:30, "He must become greater; I must become less."

Rod Handley
COO/CFO, Fellowship of Christian Athletes

The Fellowship of the Unashamed

Romans 1:16

I am a part of the "**Fellowship of the Unashamed.**" I have the Holy Spirit Power. The die has been cast. I have stepped over the line. The decision has been made. I am a disciple of Jesus Christ. I won't look back, let up, slow down, back away or be still. My past is redeemed, my present makes sense, and my future is secure. I am finished and done with low living, sight-walking, small planning, smooth knees, colorless dreams, tame visions, mundane talking, chintzy giving and dwarfed goals!

I no longer need pre-eminence, prosperity, position, promotions, plaudits or popularity. I don't have to be right, first, tops, recognized, praised, regarded or rewarded. I now live by presence, lean by faith, love by patience, lift by prayer and labor by power.

My pace is set, my gait is fast, my goal is Heaven, my road is narrow, my way is rough, my companions few, my Guide reliable, my mission clear. I cannot be bought, compromised, deterred, lured away, turned back, diluted or delayed. I will not flinch in the face of sacrifice, hesitate in the presence of adversity, negotiate at the table of the enemy, ponder at the pool of popularity or meander in the maze of mediocrity.

I won't give up, back up, let up or shut up until I've preached up, prayed up, paid up, stored up and stayed up for the cause of Christ. I am a disciple of Jesus Christ. I must go until He returns, give until I drop, preach until all know and work until He comes.

And when He comes to get His own, He will have no problem recognizing me. My colors will be clear.

1

A Call To Accountability

For several years I have shared how being accountable has changed my life. Reactions I've received from a great number of people have ranged from "What is it?" to "I'm already doing that too!" Yet, no matter what the initial reaction, once I begin sharing what my accountability group does and how we do it, I see their expressions and more than one has said, "This is something I need so badly in my life."

I became interested in accountability because of two primary reasons. The first one was personal. Though I had an impressive address and phone book listing and could mix fairly well in most social situations, I found myself longing to have someone who knew me for who I really was, and would be willing to listen, advise and challenge me to live in an upright godly manner. John 15:13 says, "Greater love has no one than this, that he lay down his life for his friends." I did not have this type of friend. I also knew there were areas of my life where I needed greater obedience to the Lord and I needed someone to help me follow through with my commitments. I was also dissatisfied with the surface and shallow conversations in which I so often found myself engaging, even with those who were supposed to be my closest friends.

The second reason I became interested in accountability was the pattern of failures which I observed in the lives of many Christians whom I admired and followed closely. When I speak of failure, I am referring to public and private sin which seriously damaged their ministry or job, reputation, families and relationship with God. As I began to ask questions, I discovered that many of those who fell had no accountability in their life.

Among those who had fallen was a pastor who led seminars across the country while secretly engaging in an adulterous relationship for a number of years. According to a person close to the situation, just prior to beginning this affair, he removed himself from any form of accountability because he felt he was self-sufficient; it was too time consuming and unnecessary.

Another sharp, young pastor whom I respected greatly because of his Bible-based preaching style, was dismissed from his church when it was discovered he had inappropriate relationships with women in his congregation. A reason cited for his fall was a lack of accountability.

A business leader and deacon in a local church who had been named the "Man of the Year" in his community was recently found guilty of embezzling millions of dollars from various people and several charitable organizations. He was an investment advisor and people placed their trust in him. Again, a lack of accountability was noted in his life.

Even the person who played a key part in my Christian faith stumbled. A victim to the temptations of the world in the areas of prosperity, career and success, he is now barely hanging on to the faith in Christ which he had vibrantly exposed to me. Apparently, there was no one in his life who walked beside him in an accountable relationship.

In each of these cases I do not believe there was an intentional desire to fall. Genuine Christians want to live an obedient life to Jesus Christ. Yet, temptations are real and powerful. No person has the ability to always make the right decisions. Unfortunately, poor choices result in terrible consequences, no matter how innocent the initial decision might have been.

Examples of people who have fallen are not isolated. Unfortunately almost every day people are falling away from Jesus Christ and destroying many loved ones as sin is exposed. The stark reality is each and every one of us, including myself, is capable of falling. We are not exempt from the possibilities of stumbling, and every Christian needs some form of accountability in his or her life.

Many people are unwilling to answer to anyone! Such reasons include: lack of time, a desire to maintain privacy, mistrust with others primarily due to past hurts, a fear of rejection, a secret pattern of sin and an unwillingness to get help, just to name a few.

But the weak spots and other areas where we are blinded usually are the places where we are attacked by temptation. Though some may fall abruptly due to one single bad decision, most of those who get into trouble make a series of tiny bad decisions-even decisions which go undetected-that slowly wear down the character of a person. Song of Solomon 2:15 talks about the "little foxes that ruin the vineyard." These foxes may include areas where we are totally off base. At other times the foxes may be a slight compromise which goes unchallenged by anyone in our lives. God's Word teaches us to stand firm in the faith and to guard against falling away (Hebrews 5:14). Unfortunately, many fall away because they do not have to answer to anyone for their behavior. Is there anyone in your life asking you hard questions about the real issues which you face on a daily basis?

The dictionary defines accountability as "subject to the obligation to report, explain or justify something; being responsible or answerable to someone."

Before going any further let me remind us that we are all sinners. Romans 3:23 says, "For all have sinned and all fall short of the glory of God." All means everyone, so whether we are a Christian or not, we all have sin in our lives. For the Christian, Jesus Christ's shed blood on the cross covers that sin, and fortunately even when sin abounds, grace abounds even more. We are forgiven and start anew and afresh at any time because God truly forgives and restores anyone who confesses and repents. For those who have not made a decision to follow Christ yet, that same love and forgiveness is available to you at anytime.

My prayer is that we all hate sin as much as God hates sin. You have probably heard the phrase, "Hate sin but love the sinner." I believe the definition of accountability described above is a practical step in staying away from the sin that so easily tempts us. Remember, accountability will not remove sin or keep you from sin, but it helps you to become aware of your sin and helps point and focus you back on Jesus Christ. Being accountable takes honesty, and if it doesn't exist, it will be a meaningless experience.

We are kidding ourselves if we think we can run the Christian race of faith alone. Scripture shows us clearly that God designed us to be in relations with one another. Certainly there are times when we must walk alone and be a bright, shining light to the world when possibly no one else will join us. Yet we all need a person of refuge who is committed to helping restore, equip and teach us to walk in the path He has set before us.

Though each person will face a different battle, many men and women are tempted by sexual passions. We are bombarded by television and movies; by books and magazines we read or browse; through the lust of the eyes. It leads to inappropriate behavior of sexual gratification outside of marriage. I have no idea of the percentage of men and women who seriously battle this one issue, yet it is clearly a significant one. Still, the areas of life where we need the help of another are not limited to sexual purity.

For men our areas of struggle include: power, success, a desire to accumulate wealth, job situations, and ego among others. Women are faced with some of these identical problems and many others as well. The issue of poor self images is one which both men and women battle. In these areas it drags us away from loving and serving the Lord totally as our Christian walk becomes shallow, legalistic, meaningless and eventually non-existent.

CHRIST, OUR PROVIDER

Certainly, Jesus Christ walks by our side on a daily basis simply because He has promised to do so. Are you aware of this promise? Robert Boyd Munger's booklet, "My Heart-Christ's Home" gives us a beautiful picture of someone inviting Christ into their life, and Him actually entering their heart, or literally their home. It is Christ's desire to occupy every single room of our house including the secret closets. In this booklet Jesus is invited into every room of the house until one day Jesus discovers the "Hall Closet." As He does, He also volunteers to clean it out. No matter what sin or what pain there might be in the past, Jesus is ready to forgive, to heal and to make whole.[1]

Our desire to be accountable to Him and others should come as a result of desiring to be more like Him. Submitting our lives for inspection goes against our independent desires and an attitude of keeping things between "me and Jesus." But Scripture points us to a need for accountability in Ecclesiastes 4:9-10, "Two are better than one, because they have a good return for their work: If one falls down, his friend can help him up. But pity the man who falls and has no one to help him up!"

WHY DO WE NEED TO BE ACCOUNTABLE?

1. *Satan, our enemy, loves to see us stumble.*

"Be self-controlled and alert. Your enemy the devil prowls

around like a roaring lion looking for someone to devour. Resist him, standing firm in the faith, because you know that your brothers throughout the world are undergoing the same kind of sufferings." (1 Peter 5:8-9)

"Put on the full armor of God so that you can take your stand against the devil's schemesmay be able to stand firm against the schemes of the devil." (Ephesians 6:11)

It brings great pleasure to Satan to see us fall, especially those who are in leadership positions in the Body of Christ. Yet every believer is a target. Satan has many methods, but two of his favorite and trickiest ways are: (1) convincing us we can do it on our own, and (2) injecting distractions through our weakest areas, particularly when we have idle time on our hands. (For more on our enemy, see Chapter 6).

2. The world is closely watching us.

"In the same way, let your light shine before men, that they may see your good deeds and praise your Father in heaven." (Matthew 5:16)

"Be very careful, then, how you live—not as unwise but as wise, making the most of every opportunity, because the days are evil." (Ephesians 5:15-16)

"Let us not become weary in doing good, for at the proper time we will reap a harvest if we do not give up." (Galatians 6:9)

First of all, God commands us to be holy because He is holy (1 Peter 1:16). Second, it is important that we remain pure and holy because of the great example it is to a watching world. It is true that you are the only Jesus that some people may ever see. Obviously we are not perfect, but when we live in obedience to Christ, people will take notice. Perhaps they might even be attracted to a relationship with Christ by observing our actions and hearing our words.

One example is Billy Graham. Billy has been used and blessed by the Lord since he burst into the public eye over 50 years ago in the early days of the "Youth for Christ" movement. Early in his ministry he and a group of men made a commitment to one another that they would remain faithful to their spouses and have integrity in all their affairs. To a watching world, he has certainly made a difference in many lives.

3. To remain right with the Lord.

"But because of his great love for us, God, who is rich in mercy, made us alive with Christ even when we were dead in transgressions—it is by grace you have been saved. And God raised us up with Christ and seated us with him in the heavenly realms in Christ Jesus, in order that in the coming ages he might show the incomparable riches of his grace, expressed in his kindness to us in Christ Jesus. For it is by grace you have been saved, through faith—and this not from yourselves, it is the gift of God—not by works, so that no one can boast. For we are God's workmanship, created in Christ Jesus to do good works, which God prepared in advance for us to do." (Ephesians 2:4-10)

As these Scriptures describe, God has done a complete work in us. Why blow it? There are many reasons to keep the relationship intact. First, He loves us. This love has been demonstrated to us time and time again, even when we fail miserably in returning that love to Him. His love for us is further demonstrated by God's willingness to send Jesus to the earth to die for us (Romans 5:8). He paid a significant price for us through His shed blood, and we have the opportunity to spend eternity with Him by accepting Christ into our life. When we also consider His power and forgiveness in our life, I continue to ask: Why blow it? Living pure, holy and blameless should be a goal for every believer.

4. It encourages other believers and ourselves.

"Brothers, if someone is caught in a sin, you who are spiritual should restore him gently. But watch yourself, or you also may be tempted. Carry each other's burdens, and in this way you will fulfill the law of Christ. Therefore, as we have opportunity, let us do good to all people, especially to those who belong to the family of believers." (Galatians 6:1,2,10)

Most people don't have close friends—they have work friends or golf partners. Our culture discourages closeness. The typical male is taught to be: autonomous, efficient, goal oriented, disconnected to people, unemotional and self-sufficient. It is a wonderful feeling to gather with people who really love and accept you and are willing to talk to you honestly and help keep you on the "straight and narrow" path. One of the members of our group shared that because of our group he loves Jesus Christ more than ever because the group helped him draw closer to Christ. As we laugh, cry and pray together, not only are our relationships strengthened, but we also love Jesus more.

WHAT HAPPENS TO US WHEN WE ARE ACCOUNTABLE?

1. Growth in your Christian walk.

Opening yourself to others will result in a great time of personal growth. You will be challenged and encouraged in a multitude of ways in trusting God with your whole heart (Jeremiah 29:11-13). Knowing we do not face the battles of daily life and spiritual growth alone matters a great deal. Though your group may not have any members with a counseling degree, a willing listener and a prayer partner can be extremely comforting. Dietrich Bonhoeffer said, "Many people are looking for an ear that will listen...they do not find it among Christians, because these Christians are talking where they should be listening...one who cannot listen long and patiently will presently be talking beside the point and be never really speaking to others."[2] To find people who can listen long and patiently is like discovering a treasure.

2. Deepening Friendships.

Not only will the depth of the friendships increase in your group, but you will find it easier to develop solid, meaningful friendships outside of the group because you will initiate conversations beyond normal surface issues (Philippians 1:27). As you feel love and acceptance from your group, it frees you up in your other friendships to be yourself.

3. Greater Awareness.

Because you will discuss real issues, it will open your eyes to the needs and situations of everyday life including family situations, church involvement, integrity, half-truths and a variety of other issues. (1 Corinthians 16:13-14). The simple act of sharing the raw material of daily life with an accountability group helps in seeing situations through the eyes of others. It keeps attention focused and constantly reminds us to pray. James Houston of Regent College says, "Sin always tends to make us blind to our own faults. We need a friend to stop us from deceiving ourselves that what we are doing is not so bad after all. We need a friend to help us overcome our low self-image, inflated self-importance, selfishness, pride, our deceitful nature, our dangerous fantasies and so much else."[3]

4. *Priority Setting.*

When our hectic schedules crowd out time for prayer, family relationships, or exercise, we need people to remind us that the tasks that seem so urgent are not worth the compromise. These friends can help balance competing demands and bring choices into harmony with the life taught and modeled by Scripture. It will also give you a place to apply action to what you are learning.

5. *Peace.*

How would you feel if Christ returned and you were in the midst of an embarrassing situation? This is a good question to ask yourself when you encounter situations which may not be appropriate. 1 John 2:28 says, "And now, dear children, continue in him, so that when he appears we may be confident and unashamed before him at his coming."

A sense of personal satisfaction and joy are a few of the emotions which will begin to make a difference in your private world. What a feeling to have the freedom to let other people participate with you in releasing your burdens to Christ (Matthew 11:28-30).

Have you ever been to the Redwood Forest in Northern California? Here you see impressive trees which are hundreds of feet high and extremely thick. Most trees of this size have a root system which is equal to what you see above the surface. Not redwoods. Although their root system is only a few feet deep, they survive the storms and wind because they grow next to other redwoods, and their root systems become incredibly strong by binding together with one another. They do not topple because of their mutual support.

Being in a accountability group will provide this type of a support system.

THE DIFFERENCE BETWEEN ACCOUNTABILITY AND FELLOWSHIP

It all comes down to an openness to asking and answering the hard questions. Typically fellowship never gets beyond the routine conversations of news, sports and weather. Accountability pushes into the real issues of life. You may from time to time even get to the point where you have to push into areas where you may endanger your friendship because of a mutual commitment to one another. Challenging, probing discussions are invited into the conversation. Typically, fellowship never gets this intimate.

"QUIET QUALITIES OF THE MIGHTY MEN OF GOD"

I Resolve To Be Like...

ENOCH...walk with God and please Him.
DAVID...to be a man after God's own heart.
ABRAHAM...believe in God and be reckoned as righteous.
JEHOSAPHAT...prepare my heart to seek God.
MOSES...choose to suffer rather than enjoy the pleasures of sin.
NOAH...stand alone even while being mocked.
DANIEL...commune with God at all times.
JOB...be patient under all circumstances.
GIDEON...stand firm even though friends are few.
AARON...uphold the hands of my spiritual leaders.
ISAIAH...consecrate myself to the Lord's work.
JOHN...lean on the bosom of Christ.
STEPHEN...forgive those who hurt me.
BARNABUS...seek to be an encourager to others.
PAUL...forget what lies behind and press on.
JESUS CHRIST...delight to do the will of the Father.
THE HEAVENLY HOST...proclaim the glory of the Lord.

List compiled by Rod Handley from various Scriptures.

[1] Robert Boyd Munger, *My Heart-Christ's Home* (Downers Grove, IL: Inter-Varsity Christian Fellowship, 1986 revised).
[2] Christianity Today, March 11, 1991, page 44.
[3] Christianity Today, March 11, 1991, page 43.

2

A Look at Our Group

In early 1990, shortly after moving to Kansas City, I met Steve Mogensen. Through Steve I became interested in meeting in a small group on a weekly basis. As a new believer he was seeking Christian fellowship. With Steve's encouragement four of us began meeting together at a local restaurant once a week for a time of updates and prayer. It was a positive time, yet had little structure. Since we were all single, it met some common needs, both social and spiritual.

Accountability took on a new meaning and was raised to a higher level when I began meeting with a second group of men in the fall of 1990. Along with my roommate Steve Pelluer and Kansas City Chiefs teammate Ken Karcher, we began getting together three times a week. In addition to answering a set of personal questions which had been provided by Athletes in Action director Mike Lasardi, we also made a commitment to memorizing Scripture together. Our goal was to memorize the entire book of 2 Timothy. By Christmas 1990 all three of us had the book memorized, and together forged an incredible friendship.

With their help I experienced some of the most meaningful conversations during these months. We got beyond the surface areas, down to some of the nitty gritty issues about myself which was historically off limits to everyone in my life.

I was scared that if someone really got to know me, perhaps they would not want to be my friend. It wasn't necessarily that I was bad or evil, but I was afraid of people seeing my flaws and judging my imperfections. I understand now that the fears were totally unfounded. As I opened up to Steve and Ken, I discovered that they accepted me and loved me more than before because of my openness. I also found that they too had areas of struggles in their life, and they could identify with my weaknesses. No longer were we single islands, trying to fight this battle alone. We could help one another strive toward godly living.

When I began sharing with others about our accountability group, I learned that many people were interested not only in the topic, but also in starting a group themselves. The only problem was how to get started. I gave them our set of questions but knew this wasn't enough. Several people suggested that I write a book on accountability.

I searched the book stores for guidance and was unable to find any resource help. I visited with Jeff Comment, President of Helzburg Diamonds and past chairman of Young Life, to find out if he knew where I could find these resources. He shared, "Rod, I know of nothing out there in published print to describe this type of accountability. I believe there are few, if any, who are willing to touch this subject because it is the one area of Christianity that is a little too close to the real person." In the same conversation he encouraged me to write a book.

The final confirmation for writing the book came when I heard the testimony of Minaz Abji, one of my current accountability partners and a member of the same church I attend. I met Minaz in March 1993 at a men's weekend retreat. By coincidence the Lord arranged for the two of us to be roommates during the weekend. On Saturday morning at the retreat were visiting together prior to breakfast, and he asked me, "How can a Christian stay away from sin?" Among other things I mentioned that my accountability group helped me. I invited him to observe our group which he did the following week. After his first week he was quickly welcomed in as a regular participant.

Several months later Minaz was asked to give his testimony to the entire church congregation. As I sat in the audience, I was overwhelmed by his story. Minaz grew up in Uganda as a Muslim. During Idi Amin's reign his family fled to Canada as refugees. While in Canada he married Julia who had grown up Buddhist. After their daughter Nadia was born, they began questioning their Muslim and Buddhist heritage and sought spiritual meaning for their life. Skeptical of "the church," they were approached by Jehovah Witnesses who knocked on their door one day. After attending Bible studies and the Jehovah Witness services for five years, they still felt uneasy about what they were hearing. On their own they went to a Christian church one day and shortly thereafter, made a first time commitment to Christ.

In Minaz's testimony I was stopped dead in my tracks when he told of the impact that our accountability group had on his life since the weekend retreat. He said, "Prior to joining this group, Christianity was good, but it was not dealing with the real issues of my life. This group has exhibited what true Christianity is all about, and now for the first time in my journey with Christ, I am seeing victories in areas where I had been defeated. And for the first time in my life I am living the Christian life." Though he had made a decision to follow Christ years before, he was truly transformed.

As he spoke, I heard the Lord saying to me, "Rod, there are people like Minaz in this world who need what you have discovered from your experiences with accountability. Write the book!"

Of course, I argued with myself that lack of time and poor writing skills were good reasons to not write a book. But along with those arguments, my mind was churning. As our pastor preached from the pulpit, I scribbled out an initial outline. When the service ended, I found Jeff Comment coming toward me. I told him about how the Lord had prompted me during the service, and he encouraged me once again to begin the writing process.

Now as you read this finished product, I can see how God has worked in a marvelous way through the men who have been part of my life to bring me farther along in my journey to become more like Christ. Here is a brief snap shot of each of them and some of their comments about accountability.

Ken Karcher: Ken left the Kansas City area in March 1991 and is currently the offensive coordinator for the University of Pittsburgh football program. He and his wife Pauline have three children under the age of five. Ken recalls, "Those nine months together with the guys were the most meaningful times in my Christian life. Since that time, I have been seeking to be part of a group and fellowship patterned after it. Our group encouraged and challenged me to live a righteous and godly life day to day. When men hold each other accountable, Christianity becomes real!"

Steve Pelluer: Steve left Kansas City in April 1992 and recently received a counseling degree from Colorado Christian College. He was married in 1994, and he and his wife Jennifer live in the Denver area. Steve recalls, "The biggest impact was facing life honestly. It was a big step in developing quality relationships."

Vic Gamble: When we first met in 1991, Vic was the courier for the Kansas City Chiefs and had dreams of going into full-time Christian work someday. Today he is in his final year of seminary. He said, "The initial introduction to accountability meant telling people what was going on in my heart. Without accountability, confessing your faults becomes routine which leads to a non-chalant and non-caring attitude. With accountability, your awareness of sin increases, and you face it head on before it becomes an even bigger problem."

He remembers several years ago during his first year in seminary when things were tight financially. The group gave him a cashier's check. He said, "That was an overwhelming experience to know that the guys who loved me the most were tangibly helping a great need." The group has also become his family. "The questions and issues we talk about are important, but the social portion is also crucial. Knowing you will see your closest friends once a week is truly a highlight. They care about you spiritually and every possible way that a family does." The group expanded and that has helped Vic handle change. "Initially I didn't like adding new members, but now I see change is good, and the status quo is not always the best." Vic has been married to Cathy for a little over a year.

Dan Meers: Dan is the mascot for the Kansas City Chiefs (alias "KC Wolf"). His wife Cam shared that she is so excited that he is part of a group because it makes her more confident of her marriage. "Because of his commitment to our marriage, being accountable is a priority to him. It is great that he meets with other men. And because I see how it has impacted him, I'm in an accountability group with two women," said Cam.

While in college Dan met with two guys weekly to share and pray with one another. Once he moved to Kansas City that was also a priority. He said, "I knew I needed the encouragement. Within our group I know I am meeting with other guys who love Jesus and have a common goal of striving to be more like Him. It is great when you are walking hand in hand together rather than by yourself."

"The accountability questions we answer each week are probing and confront areas that guys really deal with. Initially it was hard to open up and admit the weaknesses and struggles in my life. However, God has taught me that when I confess my weaknesses to the group, He uses these men to challenge and encourage me in my obedience to Christ. We constantly strive to be men of character and to live a life of purity which is a message that contradicts everything the world tells us. It has taught me to be more concerned about what God sees in my life rather than what the world says, and I'm learning to live my life for an audience of One. It has also helped my marriage through the wise counsel of others, and seeing the answers to prayer week after week has also been a great encouragement."

Steve Mogensen: As mentioned earlier, Steve approached me in the spring of 1990. During the previous year, he had committed his life to Christ and was looking for growth opportunities. A mutual friend encouraged the two of us to pursue a friendship. Steve wanted to surround himself with as many Christian men as possible. He said, "I needed encouragement to not go back to my old friends and lifestyle. I knew without other Christian men in my life, I wouldn't make it. The group enhanced my walk with Christ. Normally men in the world, even in the church, are not asking tough questions. People in this group asked me to address tough questions because they really cared." Today Steve and his wife Andrea and son live in Dallas. However, it has been hard finding men to regularly meet with due to a demanding travel schedule with his job. Steve said, "Not having a group currently is difficult, and I miss it."

William Hanna: I met William in April 1990, and he joined our breakfast group that fall. He is an attorney for Morrison & Hecker. He said, "So many people go to church or Bible study yet don't know how to apply the lessons they are taught to their lives. This group helps provide a concrete way to live out the Christian faith. Accountability serves as a barometer, and because that reading isn't always positive, accountability helps point you back in the right direction. Also, through meeting, you realize the importance of having God be in charge of all aspects of your life...not just a few of the areas. This has helped provide focus and direction to all areas of my life including my work and my marriage." William has been married to Tanya for three years and they have an infant son. She is also in a women's accountability group.

Fred Olson: Fred works with me at FCA. We have a great friendship, so it was easy to extend our relationship into an accountability group. He said, "Accountability has helped in two primary ways: (1) the enhanced friendships with other Christian guys and the closeness we feel for one another and (2) it has strengthened and encouraged me in my faith. Seeing how God works in their lives has encouraged me greatly, just as the apostle Paul mentions in 1 Thessalonians 2:12, 3:2. These kinds of deep friendships do not happen very often with guys. Also, I am much more aware of doing right and being right not only in the big things, but in the little things as well."

Mike DeBacker: Mike works for HNTB (architects, engineering and planning). He said, "The group has helped me with an overall awareness of the pure and righteous life God desires for each of us. I have also learned what it means to be faithful to God financially (tithing and debt reduction primarily). Every question we ask and the fellowship we share have meant so much. Even getting up early to make the 6:00 a.m. meeting is a real highlight. Plus, my marriage to Darla has also been greatly enhanced due to the wisdom of the other guys." Darla said, "Getting feelings out in the open with other men also results in better communication within the marriage."

Jeff Klein: After years of investigating Christianity, Jeff (Jewish by birth) made an initial decision to follow Christ in August 1993. A friend who was instrumental in Jeff's decision called me from Seattle and asked if I could help hook him up with other believers. He joined our group, and an instant bonding occurred. He said, "Direction, guidance, friendship and fellowship are key parts of our group. Telling the guys how I reacted to and applied their input helps make you very cognizant of what you are doing with your day. I guarantee you, none of us is a saint. We are all sinners, yet we are not judged according to our performance. As you talk about your feelings and various issues, you always come away better than when you arrived." He added, "Making real friends is very limited in our current society. These are quality relationships! You receive and give a lot. As a new Christian, I haven't felt like an outsider. I felt comfortable in sharing from the very beginning, even though I had a lack of knowledge and experience in my new faith. I have felt this way because they cared about me. Though I'm not necessarily qualified to give comments, I know God is using me, too. We all bring baggage and valuable input as well. Also, a highlight time is our prayer around the table. This was new to me at first, but now it's something I really enjoy." Jeff and his wife Cindy have three children, and he directs stadium operations at Arrowhead Stadium.

Kevin Harlan: Kevin moved to Kansas City to work with FCA in January 1994. He was in a group like this in Tulsa; however our format was new to him. He said, "I found in this group the accountability structure needed to live out the Christian life. As someone in ministry, I have a special calling and extra responsibility to maintain my commitment to Christ. I have seen too many ministry folks fail because there wasn't a group around them. Within this group I know I am better protected." Kevin and his wife Sharon have two sons.

Mark Zeller: Mark has been a faithful friend since I moved to Kansas City. He said, "Guys normally don't know how to communicate their feelings, even in a Bible study situation. It really does bring you together. In sharing we truly became committed to one another."

Minaz Abji: Minaz is the general manager of the Westin Crown Center and he and his wife Julia have three children. In addition to what has already been covered, he added, "I was struggling with sinful thoughts, especially in my non-Christian work environment. I didn't walk the walk in my entire life. Meeting with these men opened my eyes to my sin. I was shocked to see godly men opening up to these questions. The facades were broken down. I desired purity. I wanted to be obedient. Today Christ is at the center of my life. And for a long time I came and received, but now I can see how God is using me to make a difference in the lives of others. Every person needs a group like this. Christianity is more than going to church and reading the Bible; it is now in my heart. I am now experiencing real joy."

Each of the members in our group has made a commitment to follow Jesus Christ. We are confident that God has indeed promised us eternal life and salvation because we each have personally accepted him into our life. Have you made that decision? Before you go any further, consider asking Jesus Christ to come into your life. The following can guide you towards making this happen today.

ARE YOU SURE YOU'RE A CHRISTIAN?

The Bible says you need to do five things to become a part of God's family. If you haven't already done these, I urge you, if you're sincerely ready, to do them now:

1. **Admit** your spiritual need. "I am a sinner."
2. **Repent**. Be willing to turn from your sin, and with God's help, start living to please Him.
3. **Believe** that Jesus Christ died for you on the cross and rose again from the dead.
4. **Receive**, through prayer, Jesus Christ into your heart and life. Pray something like this from the sincerity of your heart:

"Dear Lord Jesus, I know I am a sinner. I believe You died for my sins and then rose from the grave. Right now I turn from my sins and open the door of my heart and life. I receive You as my personal Lord and Savior. Thank You for saving me. Amen."

5. Then **tell** a believing friend and a pastor about your commitment.

(Adapted from Greg Laurie, New Believer's Growth Book [Riverside, CA.: Harvest Ministries, 1985], p.8.)

3

A History and Definition of Accountability

I began this project because I was unable to find a comprehensive book devoted entirely to accountability. Some authors, like Patrick Morley in *"Man in the Mirror,"* dedicated portions of their writings to this subject, and I am grateful to Patrick for having the courage to approach this subject and give men a format to use. Much of the information which I am writing on accountability is adapted from Patrick's writings, and I encourage you to read his entire book. Steve Farrar in *"Point Man"* also does a great job of detailing some specific ways in which a man can better equip himself to be a godly man and leader.

I am also thankful for the Promise Keeper's movement which has provided a forum for men to be the types of leaders which God intended them to be and challenged me personally through their conferences. (More on the Promise Keeper's ministry in Chapter 13).

WHAT DOES SCRIPTURE SAY?

"See to it, brothers, that none of you has a sinful, unbelieving heart that turns away from the living God. But encourage one another daily, as long as it is called Today, so that none of you may be hardened by sin's deceitfulness." (Hebrews 3:12-13)

"Instead, speaking the truth in love, we will in all things grow up into him who is the Head, that is, Christ. From him the whole body, joined and held together by every supporting ligament, grows and builds itself up in love, as each part does its work." (Ephesians 4:15-16)

"And Saul's son Jonathan went to David at Horesh and helped him find strength in God." (1 Samuel 23:16)

Is Accountability a 1990's Discovery

I was surprised in my research on accountability to discover that during the mid-1700's John Wesley developed an accountability model. Wesley influenced thousands of people into Christian discipleship and growth. He said, "Preaching like an apostle without joining together those that are awakened and training them in the way of God is only begetting children for the murderer." Wesley established his converts and leaders in small cell groups for mutual care and discipling. The following are some guidelines he established for these cells. Keep in mind that these were to be followed in the spirit of the law *not* the letter of the law:

"In obedience to the command of God, by St. James and by the advice of Peter Bohler (Moravian Missionary), it is agreed by us,

1. That we will meet together once a week to confess our faults one to another, and pray one for another that we may be healed.
2. To come punctually at the hour appointed without some extraordinary reason.
3. To begin, (those of us present), exactly at the hour, with singing and prayer.
4. To speak each of us in order, freely and plainly, the true state of our souls, with the faults we have committed in thought, word, or deed, and the temptations we have felt since our last meeting."

Here are some questions people were asked before being admitted to the cell groups:

1. Have you peace with God through our Lord Jesus Christ?
2. Have you the forgiveness of your sins?
3. Has no sin, inward or outward, dominion over you?
4. Do you desire to be told of your faults?
5. Do you desire to be told from time to time whatever is in our heart concerning you?
6. Consider! Do you desire that we should tell you whatsoever we think, fear, or hear concerning you?
7. Do you desire in doing this that we should come as close as possible, that we should cut to the quick and search your heart to the bottom?
8. Is it your desire and design to be on this, and all other occasions, entirely open so as to speak everything that is in your heart without exception, without disguise and without reserve?

The following five questions were asked at every meeting:

1. What sins have you committed since our last meeting?
2. What temptations have you met with?
3. How were you delivered?
4. What have you thought, said, or done of which you doubt whether it be sin or not?
5. Have you nothing you desire to keep secret?

Wesley believed that every member should be responsible for every other member. The style of life they sought to share with each other was characterized by openness, transparency, a caring community and submission.[1]

Accountability Means "Submission"

The word "submission" often is met with suspicion. Invariably the word conjures up a picture of oppression. In contrast the Biblical meaning of submission is, "a voluntary yielding in love, a readiness to renounce one's own will for the sake of others." A couple of words help describe submission without the negatives.

The first word is *"accountability."* Accountability means I am liable to be called to account for my life. It means I am regularly answerable for key areas of my life to certain people. It means I am being held responsible for who I am and what I do. The purpose of accountability in one's life is nothing less than an attempt to become more Christ-like in our life and to grow more intimately in Him.

Because of what Jesus Christ did on the cross and our desire to serve Him totally, we are willing to submit to the scrutiny of someone else for the sole purpose of becoming more obedient and devoted to Christ. Accountability is something I *give* to others; I ask them to *hold* me accountable. Accountability is love in action as others seek to challenge me into growing toward wholeness. Accountability is the Body of Christ caring for each member—asking each one to demonstrate responsibility. It is a voluntary yielding in love. "To whom are you submitted?" is a loaded question in today's vocabulary, but "To whom are you accountable?" is an enabling question. "Submit yourselves to one another" (Ephesians 5:21) may not communicate well in today's setting, but "Be accountable to one another" says it clearly.

Groups like "Alcoholics Anonymous" who make "keep me honest pacts" between members definitely fits the accountability model. However in this example it is usually limited to just a few specific areas, where the accountability I am referring to is designed to encompass your entire life.

Has anyone ever asked you to hold them accountable for an area of their life? Have you ever asked anyone to hold you accountable in one particular area of your life? And just exactly what is accountability, anyway?

In talking with people, it is clear that accountability is a familiar term, and everyone knows it is important, but very few people actually know how to define it. This book will outline not only the principles involved in understanding accountability but also give you a mechanism for incorporating it immediately into your life.

The second word is *"interdependence."* The Body of Christ is not characterized by dependence. Dependence keeps people from wholeness. Dependence means you are unable to function as an autonomous, free agent. Dependence is crippling, not freeing.

On the other hand independence is not characteristic of the church either. We are not loners, living out a private, eccentric, aloof Christian life. It is not "God and me." Rather it is a life of interrelatedness and affirmation. We are neither dependent nor independent but interdependent. Dependence produces weak, half people. Independence produces proud, pretentious people. Interdependence produces whole, loving, serving people. Interdependence is the Body using the individual's gifts for the sake of the whole. It is the Body cooperating together in love, to see men and women coming to Christian maturity in accountable, interdependent relationships. Ephesians 4:13-15 says "Until we all reach unity in the faith and in the knowledge of the Son of God and become mature, attaining to the whole measure of the fullness of Christ. Then we will no longer be infants, tossed back and forth by the waves, and blown here and there by every wind of teaching and by the cunning and craftiness of men in their deceitful scheming. Instead, speaking the truth in love, we will in all things grow up into him who is the Head, that is, Christ."

The Need For Teamwork

As a former athlete, I participated on a number of both excellent and terrible teams. It was very easy to distinguish the difference. The poor teams were filled with individuals seeking personal gain, a lack of concern for others on the team, virtually no discipline, rampant hypocrisy and lots of backbiting and unrest. On the other hand, the good teams exhibited humility, confidence in the other members, an attitude of togetherness, a commitment to a greater cause and a belief in one another.

Teamwork is a concept which God has stressed since the beginning of time. In the Garden of Eden God saw that man and woman needed one another. Moses had his brother Aaron to help him lead people out of Egypt toward the Promised Land. David and Jonathan had a special friendship which encouraged and challenged one another then later Nathan played an important part in David's life as he was willing to confront him openly regarding his sin with Bathsheba. Daniel had his three close friends Shadrach, Meschach and Abendego to stand beside him. Paul had his special missionary companions of Barnabus, Silas and Timothy. Even Jesus Himself had His twelve disciples but a close intimate friendship with Peter, John and James. In fact, examine the Bible, and look for people who lived out their faith in God alone. You will not find anyone. Being sent out "two by two" has always been a Biblical pattern. No person can, or is meant to, live the Christian life alone. Eventually, our heart will turn towards evil. Jeremiah 17:9 says, "The heart is deceitful above all things and beyond cure. Who can understand it?"

God never intended for us to live our Christianity out as a "Lone Ranger." Even the modern day "Lone Ranger" had his sidekick Tonto and his beloved horse Silver. Today, God intends for us to not live an independent lifestyle but one of interdependence upon Himself and others around us. The embarrassing, sometimes painful, act of baring our souls to another can lead to growth.

SYNERGY

Let me explain it another way through the concept of "synergy." Synergy is one of the most powerful realities in all of God's creation. And yet it appears to be little understood and seldom practiced in the hustle and bustle of daily living. For those who learn about synergy and make it a priority in all relationships—personal, work, church, etc.—the end results and rewards will be great.

Synergy is defined as "harmonious teamwork toward a common goal to the degree that the outcome is greater than the sum of the parts." With synergy two plus two equals more than four because of the bonus effect of harmonious effort. A fire of hot coals is much hotter than the individual heat of each coal when added up. In nuclear energy the key to the awesome power is fusion or the uniting of certain elements into a chain reaction of rapid, multiple bonding or synergy.

A classic example of synergy is the two oxen of the same strength. Each one can pull four tons by itself, but together they can pull twenty-two tons. How can this be? Because of the extra adrenaline flow of having a partner in harmony in a task and because of the need to break the inertia of a non-moving weight. It is more difficult to break the inertia of the weight than to pull it. Together the oxen can break the inertia of that much weight. That same principle was tested with two horses in Germany. One horse could pull eight tons and the other one nine, but together they could pull thirty tons.

You can observe the extraordinary benefits of synergy in nature, business, athletics, the church and marriage/family relations. Wise business leaders are learning and implementing the concepts of synergy and seeing profits rise dramatically (such as Chrysler). In athletics we see heavily favored teams lose to underdogs because one worked together well as a team while the other one did not. In marriage and family synergy is critical to surviving and prospering in the pressures and trials of daily life. If a married couple is not in harmony, their prayers will be hindered, according to 1 Peter 3:7. Parents who use synergy with their children will be giving them wonderful tools for their future.

The Bible exhorts us to live in synergy with others. Exodus 18:13-27 demonstrates the benefits for Moses and the people he served. Nehemiah rebuilt the wall around Jerusalem using a synergy of many different types and ages of people who knew little or nothing about masonry. Ecclesiastes 4:9-12 illustrates the value and power of two or three together. Acts 2:22 gives a great example of synergy as the early church began to witness and minister with power and credibility. John 17 underscores the high priority for Christians to live and serve in unity, and 2 Timothy 2:2 outlines a simple plan for leadership multiplication using synergy in teaching and training.[2]

Not Such a Silly Goose

Next fall when you see geese heading south for the winter...flying along in a V formation...you might consider what science has discovered as to why they fly that way.

As each bird flaps its wings, it creates an uplift for the bird immediately following. By flying in V formation the whole flock adds at least 71 percent greater flying range than if each bird flew on its own.

People who share a common direction and sense of community can get where they are going more quickly and easily because they are traveling on the thrust of one another.

When a goose falls out of formation, it suddenly feels the drag and resistance of trying to go it alone...and quickly gets back into formation to take advantage of the lifting power of the bird in front.

If we have as much sense as a goose, we will stay in formation with those who are headed the same way we are.

When the head goose gets tired, it rotates back in the wing, and another goose flies point.

It is sensible to take turns doing demanding jobs...with people or with geese flying south.

Geese honk from behind to encourage those up front to keep up the speed. What do we say to those around us when we honk from behind?

Finally...and this is important...when a goose gets sick or is wounded by gunshots and falls out of formation, two other geese fall out with the goose and follow it down to lend help and protection. They stay with the fallen goose until it is able to fly or until it dies; and only then do they launch out on their own or with another formation to catch up with their group.

If we have the sense of a goose, we will stand by each other like that.

Author Unknown

[1] The information about John Wesley was sent to me by Craig Hamilton. The source of this is unknown although portions were taken from "Guidelines for Groups" from Broadway Baptist Church, Kansas City, Missouri.

[2] The information on synergy was compiled by FCA staff person, E.A. Gresham.

4

How To Get Started

Getting started is often the most difficult part of the entire process, because it means that you see the need for yourself to enter into an accountable (submissive) relationship. You have to be willing to set aside natural, selfish attitudes and desires and come under someone who is committed to you completely. It should not be entered into lightly but with deliberate intent and mutual commitment.

Once again I remind you that the goal is not to please others. The goal is to please God and to walk closer to Him. The apostle Paul captured the significance of this when he prayed in Ephesians 1:17, "I keep asking that the God of our Lord Jesus Christ, the glorious Father, may give you the Spirit of wisdom and revelation, so that you may know him better." The focus of spiritual friendship should never be on personality or human ingenuity but on coming to know God better. Then at the end of our life to hear Christ say, "Well done, good and faithful servant!" (Matthew 25:23)

What Does Scripture Say?

"Brothers, if someone is caught in a sin, you who are spiritual should restore him gently. But watch yourself, or you also may be tempted. Carry each other's burdens, and in this way you will fulfill the law of Christ." (Galatians 6:1-2)

"Each of you should look not only to your own interests, but also to the interests of others." (Philippians 2:4)

"A new command I give you: Love one another. As I have loved you, so you must love one another. By this all men will know that you are my disciples, if you love one another." (John 13:34-35)

"Wounds from a friend can be trusted, but an enemy multiplies kisses." (Proverbs 27:6)

"You, my brothers, were called to be free. But do not use your freedom to indulge the sinful nature; rather, serve one another in love." (Galatians 5:13)

"As iron sharpens iron, so one man sharpens another." (Proverbs 27:17)

KEYS TO GETTING STARTED

Assuming you are ready to roll, here are some guidelines to help you in finding someone to walk beside you.

1) Initially find one other person to whom you are willing to be accountable. In the working world everyone is accountable to someone. Even the self-employed owner is accountable to customers and clients. Successful businesses challenge their employees to perform certain tasks. The employee then has the opportunity to run with the goals and make things happen. With that freedom comes accurate reporting and a completed project (i.e., accountability). Unless we are accountable on a regular basis for the key areas of our personal lives, we like sheep, will go astray.

The responses we give one another should relate to the goals and standards we have set for ourselves, not contradicting Scripture. These goals should be set to help us accomplish our understanding of God's purpose for our lives and the priorities He has for us. We need someone to whom we can answer by giving an accurate report, on how we are progressing toward these goals and standards.

Finding one or more accountability partners is not easy. The overriding qualities are people who love Christ, who want to see you succeed and who also sense a need for accountability in their own lives. Pick people whom you respect, people you feel compatible with and whose judgment you trust. You do not want to end up second-guessing the person you have given authority to ask you the hard questions. Proverbs 13:20 says, "He who walks with the wise grows wise, but a companion of fools suffers harm."

You may find it more appropriate to have different people hold you accountable in different areas. Several of the guys in my group help monitor my weight. Another, I trust more with financial matters. This will take time to develop.

Chances are good that an existing friend is a candidate for an accountability partner. Those who share a common interest with you are ideal. Under no circumstance should you have a person of the opposite sex as your partner, other than your spouse. Spouses are particularly helpful in areas of personal weakness. We should invite accountability into our marriage and be willing to address all the issues with them. However, there are some things that are best shared exclusively with people of the same sex.

THE TRUTH ABOUT FRIENDS

Scripture underscores the importance of friendship by making more than one hundred references to it. Let's take a look at some truths about friends in general.

1. **Friends are essential, not optional.** There is no substitute for a friend—someone to care, to listen, to comfort, even to reprove. (Proverbs 27:6, 17)
2. **Friends must be cultivated; they're not automatic.** "Friendship is to be purchased only by friendship. A man may have authority over others, but he can never have their heart but by giving his own."[1]

3. **Friends impact our lives; they're not neutral.** Those we are close to rub off on us, change us. Their morals and philosophies, convictions and character eventually become our own. (1 Corinthians 15:33; Psalms 1:1; Proverbs 13:20)
4. **Friends come in four classifications, not one.** As we look at the different levels of friendship, notice how the number of friends we have in each of the categories *decreases* the further down the list we go. But honesty *increases* in these friendships.

a. **Acquaintances.** Acquaintances are those with whom you have infrequent contact and shallow interaction. They don't ask deep questions but skate through the relationship on the ice of superficiality.

b. **Casual friends.** With these people you have more contact, common interests, and you feel comfortable asking more specific questions.

c. **Close friends.** With close friends you share life goals, the freedom to ask personal questions, and meaningful projects.

d. **Intimate friends.** With intimate friends you have regular contact and a deep commitment to mutual character development. You share the freedom to criticize and correct, encourage and embrace. They are your sheltering trees.[2]

2) Decide the key areas for accountability. Patrick Morley gives us insight into this area by illustrating the "Titanic and the Accountability Iceberg."

The British steamer, the Titanic, was considered by experts to be unsinkable. One of the largest sea disasters in history occurred when the Titanic struck the hidden part of an iceberg on its maiden voyage during the night of April 14, 1912. Fifteen hundred people perished as the submerged part of a mountain of ice ripped open a three-hundred-foot long gash in the hull of what was then the greatest ocean liner in the world.

An iceberg is one of nature's most beautiful and dangerous phenomena. What we see of these masses of broken-off glaciers is beautiful—like the "best foot" each of us puts forward with our friends. But only one-eighth to one-tenth of an iceberg is visible—the rest is hidden below the surface of the water. And that is where the danger lurks.

Like an iceberg, the beautiful part of our lives is that tenth or so which people can see. What's below the surface, however, is where we live our real lives—lives often hidden from the scrutiny of other Christians. The jagged subsurface edges of our secret lives often rip open our relationships and damage our spiritual lives. What is unseen and not carefully examined can sink us when we are unaccountable for those areas of our lives.

THE ACCOUNTABILITY ICEBERG

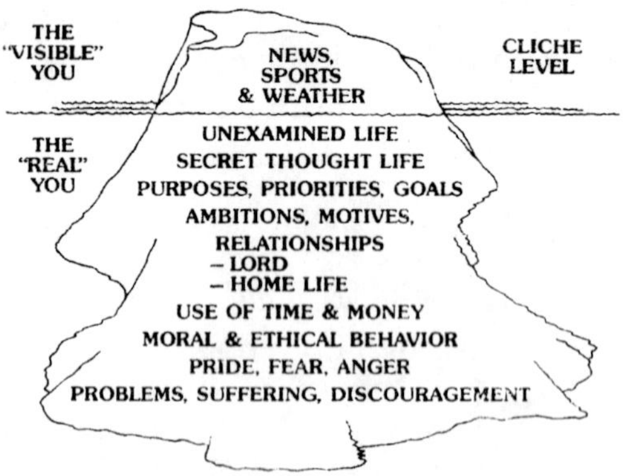

The (accountability iceberg figure) shows how most of our conversation revolves around the cliche level of life—news, sports and weather. But this is the tip of the iceberg—the "visible" you. The "real" you wrestles with gut-wrenching issues in the key areas of our lives every day, and we each need someone to help us navigate around the submerged dangers of an unexamined life. The key areas in which all of us need accountability include our: relationship with God, relationship with spouse, relationship with kids, use of money and time, moral and ethical behavior and areas of personal struggle.

What is something you really struggle with? What are your weak spots? Wouldn't you like to know your blind spots? In which areas of your secret thought life do you struggle? What are your personal areas of great temptation? These are questions an accountability partner should be asking regularly.[3]

Our accountability group has settled on ten questions which are appropriate for our needs and are noted in Chapter 5. A description of these questions are noted in Chapters 8-17. You should decide with your accountability partner(s) the best questions that fit your particular needs.

The composition of the group needs to be determined as well. In a closed group there are no visitors, and the more private the environment, the deeper you will converse. In an open group significant intimacy will not occur.

3) Set a regular time and place, including a systematic method for getting through the questions. The contact with your accountability partner(s) should be frequent. I would suggest a weekly meeting, though bi-monthly can also work. Too much happens in a month to just meet on this type of schedule. Our group gets together at 6:00 a.m. every Friday at a local restaurant. The meetings go until approximately 8:00 a.m. We spend the first few minutes getting a general update from people in the group on what has transpired over the course of the past week. Usually you can get a pretty good reading on how the specific questions will play out based on this overview time. Once everyone has had time to give his update, then we proceed into the specific questions that we have decided upon. We close our time with prayer. Here are some guidelines which have helped us.

a) Begin on time. If someone is late, then they will miss out on the general update time. A commitment to the time parameters should be followed by all members of the group. If not, it will become a source of great frustration. From time to time we have used a variety of ice-breakers to help get the time rolling. One fun way is to describe your previous week through describing a weather forecast (i.e. partly sunny, foggy, hurricane, etc.)

b) Limit the general time to just a couple of minutes per person. Though this is an important time, it should not replace the core questions. If not watched closely, you can really chew up your time talking about general, non-personal issues (i.e. news, sports and weather) during this time.

c) Have no more than four people in your group. Five or more makes it extremely difficult to get through all the questions in a timely and thorough manner. If your group is larger than four, then after the general update time, break up into smaller groups to answer the specific questions.

d) Have a different person begin each question, and juggle the order of the questions to meet the needs of your group. Initially, the questions may feel awkward, unless accompanied by personal concern, compassion and friendship. They should be asked creatively. Give the person being asked the question all the "air time" needed to give an accurate report—to "give an answer." Remember, the ultimate purpose is to become more like the Lord in all our ways. Also, allowing people to initiate the questions models leadership skills and gives everyone a sense of ownership.

e) Find your own rhythm. Each group will be different in how its members flow together. Try to eliminate all expectations. Be careful within the small group with too much structure because it can stifle the relationships.

f) Limit your comments until each person has had the chance to respond. You can really disrupt the time if you pause and analyze each response. However, be sensitive to those who need specific help or instruction in working through hardships or difficult times.

g) Keep a running list of areas where prayer requests are needed or where people make a vow to do something in the future. Once someone makes a commitment, you have an opportunity to bring this commitment to their attention at a later time.

h) Seek out and discover Biblical insights. Gain wisdom and direction from not looking for man's opinions, but on the Word of God. When direction from the Bible is not clear, refer to Chapter 5 on "gray areas."

i) Share victories as well as defeats. It's important to discuss progress in areas where historically you have stumbled. We have had lots of "high fives" during our accountability group. Greg Ponchot, Indiana Pacers chaplain, helped give me insight to this area through the illustration shown below.

	ALWAYS	SOMETIMES
WIN	4	3
LOSE	1	2

Quadrant #1 represents areas where we "always lose" pertaining to various sins/temptations in our life. Quadrant #2 is when we "sometimes lose." Quadrant #3 is when we "sometimes win." Quadrant #4 is when we "always win." We need to recognize that many times there is a process of going through all four quadrants. It may be unrealistic and extremely frustrating to assume that you or people in your group can make a jump directly from Quadrant #1 to Quadrant #4. Also, if you find yourself in the first three quadrants, you can always improve. If you are in the fourth quadrant, don't become cocky and arrogant or lest you find yourself becoming an easy prey for the enemy to attack.

j) Close in prayer. It is crucial that this be a priority for the group. Commit to pray for and encourage each other throughout the week. We also assign prayer partners on a weekly basis and encourage people to call on others to have a brief check-in time either by phone or in person. If you utilize prayer partners, juggle it around each week so that each member can build a relationship with one another.

CONFIDENTIALITY

The issue of confidentiality is a crucial one to consider. What goes on in the group must stay there. Sadly, we all have been stung by leaks of confidential information. If I am going to share the real me with someone, I want to be absolutely sure I can trust him. The fear of betrayal by a friend keeps many of us from taking the risk of being accountable. Make a covenant with your partners to assure yourself and them of the commitment you have made to confidentiality.

George Toles has been meeting with a group of three men since 1984. He says, "Each person has the right to be non-spiritual. After all, if you can't be honest here, can you be honest anywhere?" They have adopted the attitude of allowing each other to slide but to never drop the reigns on one another. He adds, "Our group doesn't get stale because we discover new caves and caverns of undiscovered information."

STAYING WITH IT

I also encourage you to stick it out. You will want to quit, perhaps often. Ask God to strengthen you when you want to give up. The purpose of accountability is to each day become more Christ-like in all of our ways. Remember, it is Jesus who is the object of our search, our devotion, our sacrifice and our affection.

If you find that you are bogging down, then I encourage you to address the concerns openly and try to determine a new course of action which will meet the needs of the group. A group could improve with a new location, time, group members, different structure or a variety of other commitments.

From time to time, you will have people leave your group both voluntarily and involuntarily. Regardless of how they leave, it is very important to maintain the confidentiality. It would be terrible to have people who left the group to discover leaks of information after not being in the group.

Adding New Members

As people move on and new people arrive, we have found it very encouraging to bring in new members from time to time. That has proved to be extremely beneficial because it brings a new energy to the group as well as a fresh perspective. A key to this success is bringing them up to speed with the rest of the group.

Dealing with Conflict

There may be times where you have a disagreement or conflict within the group. I encourage you to use the principles as outlined in Matthew 18:15-17. The ultimate goal is reconciliation by following Biblical principles. 1 Peter 5:2-3 reminds us, "Be shepherds of God's flock that is under your care, serving as overseers—not because you must, but because you are willing, as God wants you to be; not greedy for money, but eager to serve, not lording it over those entrusted to you, but being examples to the flock."

OUTSIDE THE MEETING

Look for opportunities to support one another by getting together outside of the normal meeting time. This could be dropping by the work place, having lunch/dinner together, doing a recreational activity or attending an event together.

One of the highlights of our group is an annual weekend retreat at the Lake of the Ozarks. We schedule the event months in advance and bring along our spouses and children. It is a wonderful time to enhance the relationships.

COVENANT RELATIONSHIPS

Covenant means: to agree, to be of one mind, to come together. A binding and solemn agreement to do or keep from doing. The dynamics of a covenant relationship are noted below. I encourage you to adopt these as general guidelines within your own group.

1. THE COVENANT OF AFFIRMATION (Unconditional love): There is nothing you have done, or will do, that will make me stop loving you. I will love you and affirm you no matter what you have said or done in your past. I may not agree with your actions, but I will love you unconditionally. I love you as you are and for what Christ wants to make of you. (1 John 4:7-12)
2. THE COVENANT OF AVAILABILITY: Anything I have—time, energy, wisdom, myself, finances—are all at your disposal. As part of this availability I pledge regularity of time both in prayer and meeting at agreed upon times. I consider that time to be of the highest priority on my schedule. (Hebrews 10:25)
3. THE COVENANT OF PRAYER: I promise to pray for you, to uphold you, and to attempt to listen to the Holy Spirit concerning your needs so that I can share them with you. I believe that God desires for me to pray for you. (James 5:13-16)

4. THE COVENANT OF OPENESS: I will strive to be open and transparent. I need you, and I trust you with my needs. I affirm your worth to me as a person I can trust. (2 Corinthians 6:11-13)
5. THE COVENANT OF SENSITIVITY: Even as I desire to be known and understood by you, I covenant to be sensitive to you and your needs to the best of my ability. (Galatians 6:2,10)
6. THE COVENANT OF HONESTY: I will be honest in what I think I am hearing you say and feel. If this means risking pain for either of us, I will trust our relationship enough to take that risk, realizing that it is in "speaking the truth in love" that we grow up in every way. (Ephesians 4:15-16)
7. THE COVENANT OF CONFIDENTIALITY: What goes on in this group stays here. I will say nothing that may be traced back or that could be injurious or embarrassing to my covenant partners. The assurance of confidentiality is vital to the success of the group. (1 Corinthians 1:10)
8. THE COVENANT OF ACCOUNTABILITY: You have the right to expect growth from me so that I may apply the fullness of the gifts which God has given me and fulfill my God created purposes. You have my permission to ask me about the goals I set with God, my family and my world. I expect you to lovingly not "let me off the hook." On the basis of Proverbs 27:17, "As iron sharpens iron, so one man sharpens another," I ask you to please share with me areas in my life that do not reflect Jesus because I want to grow in personal holiness. (Hebrews 10:24)
9. THE COVENANT OF FRIENDSHIP: A covenant relationship is a decision to develop friendships based on unconditional love. (Proverbs 18:24)
10. THE COVENANT OF NURTURE: It takes a conscious effort to nurture an authentic interest in others. This group forces you to do that. (Philippians 2:3-8)

11. THE COVENANT OF PATIENCE: We know that it will always take time—often a long time—to understand one another. There is no such thing as an "instant accountability group." Yet our current society, accustomed to the "instant," sometimes causes us to give up and quit before the group has time to develop. (1 Corinthians 13:4-5)

12. THE COVENANT OF EQUALITY: We will treat others as equals. The spiritual maturity, gifts and life experiences that each member brings to the group are all valid. There are no "leaders" in a covenant group. (Galatians 3:28)

13. THE COVENANT OF LISTENING: Because there are always those in a group who talk more—and those who tend to be quiet—a group requires a commitment to learn how to listen. (Proverbs 18:2; 19:27)

14. THE COVENANT OF UNANSWERED QUESTIONS: A commitment to an accountability group does not necessarily mean that if you bring a dilemma to the group, they will always provide an answer before you leave. Sometimes they are simply there to care and say, "I don't know the answer, I don't know what you should do, but I care and I will pray." (Philippians 4:6-7)

Adapted from materials provided by Dale D. Schlafer, "A Serious Call to Christian Leaders for a Devout and Holy Life" at the 1993 Promise Keepers Conference in Boulder, Colorado.

[1] Thomas Wilson, in *Speaker's Encyclopedia of Stories, Quotations, and Anecdotes*, by Jacob M. Braude (Englewood Cliffs, NJ: Prentice-Hall, 1955), p. 155.

[2] Charles R. Swindoll, *David A Man After God's Own Heart* (Anaheim, CA: Insight for Living, 1992), pp. 129-130.

[3] Patrick M. Morley, *A Man in the Mirror* (Nashville, TN: Thomas Nelson Publishers, 1992) pp. 276-277.

5

Developing Your Questions

Every group must determine the areas where accountability needs to take place. Our group has developed ten questions which work for us, but certainly each group should develop their own plan to address the areas of need. Over the past few years, I have seen a number of different formats and series of questions. Here are our ten questions.

Our theme verse is, "Therefore, brethren, be all the more diligent to make certain about His calling and choosing you; for as long as you practice these things, you will never stumble." (2 Peter 1:10 NASB)

1. Have you spent daily time in Scriptures and in prayer?
2. Have you had any flirtatious or lustful attitudes, tempting thoughts,or exposed yourself to any explicit materials which would not glorify God?
3. Have you been completely above reproach in your financial dealings?
4. Have you spent quality relationship time with family and friends?
5. Have you done your 100% best in your job, school, etc.?
6. Have you told any half truths or outright lies, putting yourself in a better light to those around you?
7. Have you shared the Gospel with an unbeliever this week?

8. Have you taken care of your body through daily physical exercise and proper eating and sleeping habits?
9. Have you allowed any person or circumstance to rob you of your joy?
10. Have you lied to us on any of your answers today?

The last question is not only a fun one, but helps remind everyone that the things shared must be done in complete honesty. If you are not going to be honest with your accountability partners, the entire commitment is meaningless.

Each of these questions and specifics on things we discuss in our accountability group, along with helpful hints are discussed in Chapters 8-17 (Section 2).

MAKING IT A DAILY EXPERIENCE

One of the discoveries I made from answering these questions with my group was a desire to walk in purity in my day-to-day activities. Because of my long history in maintaining a journal, I make the first part of my daily recording, a summary of the following ten questions. Due to the work of Christ in my own life and the success of the accountability group during this time, these daily questions really solidified my personal commitment.

1. Did I get up at least by 6:30 a.m. and have at least 8 hours of sleep? (This question really pertained to how successful I was in getting to sleep at a decent hour the night before. As a proclaimed "late night" person, my next day's performance is significantly better if I get over the urge to stay up late).
2. Did I have "quality" time with God today, through Scripture reading and prayer time?
3. Did I write at least one letter/note of encouragement? (My good friend Mike Rohrbach introduced me to this

practice. Every day I try to write someone...family member, friend or someone whom the Lord brings to mind).

4. Did I make at least one encouraging phone call to someone? (This one is similar to #3...it may be a local or long distance call).
5. Did I have an exercise time today? (At a minimum, push ups and situps should be done).
6. Did I give 100% best at my job, and what kinds of thingsoccupied my work day? (This one ties directly into the setting of priorities).
7. Did I exhibit the qualities of a man of God (above reproach, purity in all matters, humility, servant, etc.)? (This ties back to leading a life of uprightness and integrity).
8. Did I do something which made me laugh or enjoy the day more fully? (I do not want to forget the value of doing something fun each and every day. Life is too short to not enjoy each day to the fullest).
9. Did I remove something on my procrastination list? What was it? (What a great feeling to remove something from this list).
10. Did I honor and encourage my wife and children? How? (These are the most important relationships the Lord has given me. I have the tremendous privilege to serve them with my best effort).

Many people have their own daily goal schedule. For instance, Joan Cronan, Women's Athletic Director at the University of Tennessee has a daily acronym: BELLS...The "B" stands for **B**ible reading; "E" for exercise; "L" for an encouraging **l**etter; "L" for **l**earning something; and "S" for doing a special project.

VARIATIONS FROM THESE QUESTIONS

Feel free to adjust, add/delete questions as you deem appropriate for your own group or for you personally. My wife Janna has been meeting with five other women over the past year. They have added these questions: Have you used your words to build up or tear down others or self? Have you exposed yourself or contributed to gossip? They have also adjusted our Question #6, by adding the question: Have you been committed to your words?

One group I know of focuses on three areas: faith, family and finances. Another group works individually in setting various goals, and then the group quizzes them on progress of the goals at an annual retreat. Another group has an extended update time where members have the floor in answering an open question time. I have even heard of one group where periodically they will ask one of the member's spouse to come for a period of time where they can ask direct questions to the spouse to determine how things are really going from a different perspective.

One group I know of has a written report where all members fill in the blanks for the following four questions, prior to meeting together. This allows them to get a jump start and to be prepared to think through the week prior to arriving.

1. My pain was when ______________________________.
2. My growth from last week was ____________________.
3. Growth I desire for next week is __________________.
4. My wins were _________________________________.

The key is to determine areas of your life where you need immediate and specific help. Do not run from difficult questions, instead, challenge yourself to be completely above reproach in all areas of your life and be all that God wants you to be.

FROM A WOMEN'S PERSPECTIVE

Deb Shepley says, "Being involved in an accountability group has been one of the best things that I have done as a Christian. I did not need another Bible study or fellowship group. I needed to know that people cared about me, would pray for me, encourage me, and yes, keep me accountable for areas of struggle. Our small group of five women was targeted to female coaches. All of us have grown through the experience, and though I thought I knew them before, I have learned more about them as we have shared. One morning, one shared about an eating disorder, and it brought us closer together. I have found that in my own life a great danger is in feeling I have no needs. All around me the world emphasizes self-reliance, self-help, self-expression, self-confidence, self-sufficiency. Yet, I know I need people and more importantly I need Jesus."

Deb, as well as other women, have discovered that accountability works for women as well as for men. In fact, it may be easier initially for women to address accountability issues.

GUIDELINES FOR GRAY AREAS
10 Key Questions To Ask Yourself

There may be some areas where answers may not be easy to determine, because it is not a black and white issue. I call these the "gray" areas. Here are some guidelines to consider to help you in determining the right decision to make.

1. (**Desire**) Do I honestly desire to know God's will? (John 5:30; 7:17)
2. (**Scripture**) Is there a scripture passage or Biblical principle to consider or apply? (Psalms 119:105; Mark 12:24)

3. **(Prayer)** Have I sincerely prayed and asked God about what I should do? (Jeremiah 33:3; James 1:5; John 5:14-15)
4. **(Counsel)** What is the counsel of others, especially from those who know and love me and God's Word? (Proverbs 11:14; 12:15; 15:22; 19:20)
5. **(Loving others)** Will doing this provide a loving example and build up others? (John 13:34-35; 1 Corinthians 8:9, 12; 10:24)
6. **(Effect me)** Will this help me to grow more like Christ, or could it potentially enslave me? (1 Corinthians 6:12; 10:23)
7. **(Christ)** What do I think Jesus would do about this? (1 John 2:5-6)
8. **(Witness)** Will doing this make me a more believable Christian and a better witness for Christ? (1 Corinthians 9:19-22; 10:32-33)
9. **(Glorify)** Will doing this bring greater glory to God? (1 Corinthians 10:31)
10. **(Peace)** Do I honestly have a peace about doing this? (1 Corinthians 14:33; Philippians 4:7; Colossians 3:15)

Author Unknown

6

Satan and His Strategy

When I played college football, we spent many hours watching films of our opponents, reading scouting reports, looking for patterns and tendencies and determining strengths and weaknesses. Before we stepped onto the battlefield on Saturday, we had a pretty good idea of who we were up against. Ultimately, it resulted in developing a game plan which we felt would result in victory.

In the game of life our opponent, Satan, is our enemy. In this battle Satan will be defeated by God in the end. But along the way Satan will do everything in his power to defeat us. As believers we can be successful against this opponent if we know his strategies and how to call upon the weapons of warfare to defeat him.

Who Is He?

Satan is first identified in Genesis 3:1 as a serpent, "more crafty than any of the wild animals." He distorts God's truth and leads Adam and Eve into the first sin. In Genesis 3:15 Satan receives his punishment from God as the first mention of Christ is made: "he (Jesus) will crush your head, and you (Satan) will strike his heel." Right then Satan's doom was assured, but that did not stop his destructive nature. Perhaps his stubbornness, anger, evil nature and pursuit of self was all part of the reason he decided to take as many people down with him as possible.

Isaiah 14:12-15 and Ezekiel 28:12-19 give a vivid picture of Satan's fall from heaven. Pride was in his heart. He wanted to be God. He is even described as a "marvelous creation," and, though powerful, he remains in subjection to God's power, and there is absolutely nothing he can do about it. He goes by many titles: Prince of Darkness, Beast, Destruction, Anti-Christ, Devil, Serpent, Tempter." I believe one of his greatest weaknesses is that he can't foresee the future. That is probably another reason why he is so persistent, and until Christ defeated him directly by overcoming death on the cross, he might have thought he could win. Even when Jesus showed up in the flesh, Satan was present, trying to twist God's Word (yes, even Satan knows the Bible well).

What Is He Like?

1. *A murderer and a liar, right from the beginning.* The Father of all lies. He distorts and twists the truth. He lies about God and His love for you. He is the author of conflict. He is the opposite of God in every character quality. There is nothing good in him. (John 8:44)
2. *He masquerades himself as an angel of light.* He tries to convince you that his ways are best (i.e., by promoting self first, seeking anger/revenge instead of forgiveness, murder instead of life, addictions instead of submission). He camouflages his true identity and purpose by making his ways seem appealing. Sin is Satan's agent. (2 Corinthians 11:14)
3. *A sinner from the beginning.* The author of all sin. He will do anything to get people away from God and His love. (1 John 3:8)

What Are His Strategies?

1. *At times he is blunt.* Newspaper accounts and media reports tell us that satanists, sorcerers, witches and all types of

people are roaming the world under the influence of Satan and his power. 1 Peter 5:8-9 says, "Be self-controlled and alert. Your enemy the devil prowls around like a roaring lion looking for someone to devour. Resist him, standing firm in the faith, because you know that your brothers throughout the world are undergoing the same kind of sufferings."

2. *More times he is subtle.* He is coy, attractive and very deceitful. He convinces us to compromise just a little bit as he begins to wedge his way in. He will distract us by attempting to remove God from every part of our life. He attacks areas of weakness by throwing temptations our way. He also attacks areas of strength, especially areas where we feel self-confident and where we feel we can do something alone without God's help (1 Corinthians 10:13). He will also try to cause us to doubt that God exists, and he is the king of procrastination. He will always try to get you to begin something tomorrow that should be started today.

Regardless of his method, his goal is to deceive, destroy, rule and accuse. He will do whatever is necessary to accomplish his goals.

WHAT ARE WE TO DO?

1. *Put on the full armor of God.* We have been equipped with offensive and defensive weapons which will help us extinguish his fiery darts. Prayer and knowing God's Word minimize his effectiveness. We can call upon His power to aid you in the battles we face. (Ephesians 6:10-18)

2. *Trust God.* Believe that God will be true to His Word. He has promised us that He will never leave us, nor forsake us. No matter what you face, stay close to Jesus Christ. What a Savior!

3. *Don't Get Isolated.* My good friend Ralph Stewart uses a soccer illustration. He says, "One tactic of an offensive-minded soccer team is to get a player isolated one-on-one against

the goalie. At this point he has an excellent chance to score. Satan tries a similar attack on God's people. If he can get the Christian separated from the encouragement of fellow believers, the Christian is weakened. Satan makes us feel alone in the battle when we get isolated from other believers."

REMEMBER, WE WIN!!

1. God is still in total control. 1 John 4:4 says, "You, dear children, are from God and have overcome them, because the one who is in you is greater than the one who is in the world." No matter how bad things may appear, Satan is in subjection to Almighty God. Don't lose heart or become overwhelmed with feelings of defeat. We are the victors!
2. Satan and his faithful will receive their due. Matthew 13:49-50 predicts, "This is how it will be at the end of the age. The angels will come and separate the wicked from the righteous and throw them into the fiery furnace, where there will be weeping and gnashing of teeth." Revelation 20:10 elaborates, "And the devil, who deceived them, was thrown into the lake of burning sulfur, where the beast and the false prophet had been thrown. They will be tormented day and night for ever and ever." I want a front row seat at this event. The turmoil and pain he has caused so many will finally be poured out upon him for eternity.

If I Were The Devil

If I were the Prince of Darkness...I'd want to engulf the whole world in darkness, and I'd have a third of its real estate and four-fifths of its population...but I wouldn't be happy until I had seized the ripest apple on the tree; so I'd set out however necessary to take over the United States.

I'd subvert the churches first; I'd begin with a campaign of whispers; with the wisdom of a serpent I would whisper to you as I whispered to Eve, "Do as you please." To the young I would whisper that the Bible is myth. I would convince them that man created God instead of the other way around; I would confide that what's bad is good and what's good is square...the old I would teach to pray after me, "Our Father which art in Washington."

And then I'd get organized. I'd educate authors in how to make lurid literature exciting so that anything else would appear dull and uninteresting; I'd threaten TV with dirtier movies and vice-versa; I'd peddle narcotics to whom I could; I'd sell alcohol to ladies and gentlemen of distinction...I'd tranquilize the rest with pills. If I were the devil.

I'd soon have families at war with themselves, churches at war with themselves, and nations at war with themselves until each in its turn was consumed; and with promises of higher ratings, I'd have mesmerizing media...fanning the flames.

If I were the devil, I'd encourage schools to refine young intellects but neglect to discipline emotions, just let those run wild, until before you knew it, you'd have to have drug-sniffing dogs and metal detectors at every school house door. Within a decade I'd have prisons overflowing, I'd have judges promoting pornography; soon I could evict God from the courthouse, then from the schoolhouse, and then from the houses of Congress, and in His own churches I would substitute psychology for religion and deify science. I would lure priests and pastors into misusing boys and girls and church money. If I were the devil, I'd make the symbol of Easter an egg and the symbol of Christmas a bottle.

If I were the devil, I'd take from those who have and give to those who want it until I had killed the incentive of the ambitious. And what'll you bet I couldn't get the whole United States to promote gambling as the way to get rich. I would caution against extremes in hard work, in patriotism, in moral conduct. I would convince the young that marriage is old- fashioned...that swinging is more fun, that what you see on TV is the way to be, and thus I could undress you in public...and I could lure you into bed with diseases for which there is no cure.

In other words, if I were the devil, I would just keep right on doing what he's doing. Paul Harvey....good day (from his broadcast on March 8, 1993)

7

FCA: An Accountability Model

For over forty years the Fellowship of Christian Athletes (FCA) has presented to athletes and coaches the Gospel of Jesus Christ. FCA has grown into the largest, small group, youth-oriented ministry in schools across America. It has sought to primarily serve young people and coaches, undergirded by God's Spirit operating in the lives of available people.

The first available person was Don McClanen, a student at Oklahoma State University, in whose mind the FCA concept germinated in 1947. Don spoke for three minutes in a program on "Making My Vocation Christian" and got an idea: Why not utilize the hero worship of the athlete to spotlight the greatest product of all—Christianity?

McClanen's dream was nurtured over the years, and as he prayed and contacted other individuals such as Branch Rickey, Dan Towler, Roe Johnston, Donn Moomaw, Dr. Louis Evans, Sr., Carl Erskine and others, his dream became a reality. It all came together formally on November 12, 1954, when the by-laws were adopted. Four decades later this movement continues as athletes and coaches across the country meet regularly in FCA Huddles and attend FCA Summer Camps to explore and deepen their relationship with Christ, their family, their church, their teammates and others.

HOW DOES THIS FIT INTO ACCOUNTABILITY?

For adults, the FCA Adult Chapter is a wonderful way to incorporate the accountability model. In addition to answering the questions, it also gives them an outlet for service to the youth of the community.

For youth, the FCA Huddle and Camp programs are places where they can relate intimately with peers and challenge one another to grow stronger in the faith. Specifically, FCA has developed a program called "One Way 2 Play." This program is designed to help students withstand peer pressure through choosing to lead a drug/alcohol-free lifestyle. It is built as follows:

F - Faith in Jesus Christ. We believe God forgives us, gives us the wisdom to make good decisions and the strength to carry them out. Without faith in Christ, the commitments and accountability following would be shouldered by your own ability and not on God's strength.

C - Commitment to say NO! to alcohol and drugs. A pledge to be strong in the commitment and to help others be strong, too.

A - Accountability to one another. Hard questions are regularly asked by members who make the pledge to be drug/alcohol-free through the use of positive peer pressure.

* Are you living and playing alcohol and drug-free?
* Are you encouraging others to live and play that way?
* Are you being honest with at least one mature person about your feelings and temptations?
* Are you trusting Christ to meet your needs?
* Are you honoring Him in your thoughts, words and actions?

WHO IS FCA?

They are a Christ-centered ministry who is Biblically based, helping people know and grow in Christ through the local church. The target audience is the junior high, high school and college campuses across the United States. Every FCA meeting (for coaches, athletes or adults) should be a comfortable place for the honest inquirer as well as the mature Christian.

FCA's longevity is due to the diligence of thousands of faithful volunteers throughout the country. While the staff has grown tremendously, volunteers are still the backbone of the ministry. It has been stated that 96% of all Americans participate in or watch an athletic event every week. Athletics is a powerful venue in which to impact the world for Christ.

In his book, *The Coming Revolution in Youth Ministry*, Mark Senter, III, Ph.D., analyzes the structure of several youth ministries and their method for accomplishing their purpose and mission. Dr. Senter writes, "At the end of the decade of the 1980's, FCA had regular contact with students on more campuses than the next three largest parachurch youth ministries combined. The strength of the organization (FCA) is a dedicated core of volunteer Huddle group leaders who invest their spare time. The linkage is a natural one. Coaches, or people connected with high school athletic programs, invite male and female athletes to participate in group meetings where the language of sports is mixed with the Word of God. The organization (FCA) did not need to be highly visible in order to pay staff members to work on a particular campus because a willing worker was already in place."[1]

WHAT DOES FCA DO?

The stated purpose is to "present to athletes and coaches,

and all whom they influence, the challenge and adventure of receiving Jesus Christ as Savior and Lord, serving Him in their relationships and in the fellowship of the church." The bottom line is that FCA is presenting the Gospel message through the influence of athletics and calling people to make a decision to follow Christ and serve Him. They work primarily through four areas:

1. Camps: A week of "inspiration and perspiration" for athletes and coaches with their families through a solid camping program. Speakers, including high profile coaches and athletes, challenge campers to a deeper relationship with Christ so they can return home and become influences for Christ in their schools and communities.

2. Huddles: The backbone of the school-year program, giving athletes a positive peer group to nurture Christian growth, and service. FCA Huddles are student-initiated and student-led groups of athletes and coaches who meet regularly, some on school campuses, others in homes or other meeting places. With Christ as the center of the meeting, and using the Bible as the authority, they are inspired spiritually.

3. Adult Chapters: For adults (male and female), fellowship and spiritual growth is provided while also giving FCA's huddles stability through personal and financial resources. Teams have booster clubs. FCA Huddles have Adult Chapters. Business people, pastors, FCA alumni and parents offer support by contributing time, talent and treasures. Chapter members meet to fellowship as adults and form accountability groups. They help at local events, raise funds for Huddle resources and Camp scholarships, or may provide refreshments for a weekly Huddle meeting. They provide help and encouragement for Huddle Coaches and serve as excellent role models for the student-led Huddles. FCA gives the adult volunteer a great platform from which to communicate their faith and serve Jesus Christ.

4. Development: The task of staff and volunteers is to supply administrative, programmatic and financial foundations for FCA. Trusting relationships don't just happen. They develop over time. It isn't just fund raising, but friend raising.

HOW TO GET INVOLVED?

Call 1-800-289-0909 to become aware of existing Huddle and/or Adult Chapter activities in your community as well as the names of FCA staff personnel across the country. You can also write the FCA Home Office at 8701 Leeds Road, Kansas City, MO 64129. For over forty years, FCA has talked about "influence." This poem depicts that influence.

INFLUENCE

"There are little eyes upon you,
And they're watching night and day;
There are little ears that quickly
Take in every word you say;
There are little hands all eager
To do anything you do;
And a little boy who's dreaming
of the day he'll be like you.

You're the little fellow's idol;
You're the wisest of the wise,
In his little mind about you,
No suspicions ever rise;
He believes in you devoutly,
Holds that all you say and do,
He will say and do, in your way

When he's a grown-up like you.

There's a wide-eyed little fellow,
Who believes you're always right,
And his ears are always open,
And he watches day and night;
You are setting an example
Every day in all you do,
For the little boy who's waiting
To grow up to be like you."

Author Unknown

[1] Mark Senter III, Ph.D., *The Coming Revolution of Youth Ministry* (Wheaton, IL: Victor Books, 1992), pp. 27-28.

8

Daily Time With Christ

Have you spent daily time in Scriptures and in prayer?

For accountability to work best, it takes a conscious daily effort to do so. What better place to begin the routine by making sure that you have daily time with Christ. In fact, all the areas which we will address in the following chapters all go better when this one discipline is achieved.

When I was seventeen years old, I was introduced for the first time to a "Quiet Time." Though I had grown up going to church, I thought Sunday morning was when you took your dusty Bible off the shelf (if you could find it) and went to church. There were better things to do during the week than spend daily time with God.

It took the example of former college football quarterback to convince me of a need for a "Quiet Time." I saw in him excitement and enthusiasm about scheduling time with God every day. He also had an uncompromising lifestyle. He said the strength to live the Christian life was directly tied to his time with God. He told me that this was a critical part of his day, and he encouraged me to make it a daily discipline. I remember that first day I felt a sense of great accomplishment after reading the Bible for three minutes and then closing with probably a thirty second prayer. But after years of making this a regular practice, I too have discovered the importance and the excitement of spending time with Jesus Christ.

What Does Scripture Say?

Jeremiah 29:12-13 promises, "Then you will call upon me and come and pray to me, and I will listen to you. You will seek me and find me when you seek me with all your heart." Jesus' life was also characterized by earnest devotion to the Father as evidenced by His commitment to arise early in the morning to pray (Mark 1:35). The Son of God realized that even He needed daily fellowship alone with God, and it was a top priority. Now if Jesus Christ needed this time with God, isn't it obvious that we need to do so as well?

"All Scripture is God-breathed and is useful for teaching, rebuking, correcting and training in righteousness, so that the man of God may be thoroughly equipped for every good work." (2 Timothy 3:16-17)

"For the word of God is living and active. Sharper than any double-edged sword, it penetrates even to dividing soul and spirit, joints and marrow; it judges the thoughts and attitudes of the heart. Nothing in all creation is hidden from God's sight. Everything is uncovered and laid bare before the eyes of him to whom we must give account." (Hebrews 4:12-13)

"How can a young man keep his way pure? By living according to your word. I seek you with all my heart; do not let me stray from your commands. I have hidden your word in my heart that I might not sin against you...Your word is a lamp to my feet and a light for my path." (Psalm 119:9-11,105)

"And when you pray, do not be like the hypocrites, for they love to pray standing in the synagogues and on the street corners to be seen by men. I tell you the truth, they have received their reward in full. But when you pray, go into your room, close the door and pray to your Father, who is unseen. Then your Father, who sees what is done in secret, will reward you." (Matthew 6:5-6)

"Devote yourselves to prayer, being watchful and thankful." (Colossians 4:2)

"Do not be anxious about anything, but in everything, by prayer and petition, with thanksgiving, present your requests to God. And the peace of God, which transcends all understanding, will guard your hearts and your minds in Christ Jesus." (Philippians 4:6-7)

"Therefore confess your sins to each other and pray for each other so that you may be healed. The prayer of a righteous man is powerful and effective." (James 5:16)

"This is the confidence we have in approaching God; that if we ask anything according to his will, he hears us. And if we know that he hears us—whatever we ask—we know that we have what we asked of him."
(1 John 5:14-15)

WHAT IS A "QUIET TIME?"

It is time alone with God when you allow God to speak to you through the Bible and you communicate with Him in prayer praising Him, etc. This intimate time alone with God is the key to deep Christian growth and maturity. Every committed Christian has this as a core priority!

The amount of time you expend is not critical. Invest the first few minutes in preparing your heart in prayer. Then read your Bible. Pick a place to start, and then read consecutively—verse after verse, chapter after chapter. Don't race, but avoid stopping to do a Bible study on a word, thought or theological issue presented. Read for the pure joy of reading and allowing God to speak. You may want to also use a devotional book or a Bible study. The last few minutes should be set aside for prayer. Establish, renew or enliven your personal prayer time by giving God quality time before anything else calls for your attention each day. An easy way to remember a good prayer model is by using the word ACTS.

A - Adoration. A time of worshipping Him. Tell the Lord you love Him. Reflect on His greatness, His power, His majesty and sovereignty. You are simply adoring our awesome God.
C - Confession. After entering His presence and confronting His holiness, it is evident how unclean we are. Therefore, confess and be cleansed from the sin in your life. Confession comes from a root word meaning "to agree together with." It means you are agreeing with God on specific sin that you have encountered (1 John 1:9).
T - Thanksgiving. An expression of gratitude to God. Think of specific things to thank Him for: family, job, church, ministry, answered prayer and even the hardships (1 Thessalonians 5:18).
S - Supplication. This means to "ask for, earnestly and humbly." This part of your prayer time focuses on making your petitions known to Him. Ask for others, then for yourself.

SUGGESTIONS IN DEVELOPING YOUR "QUIET TIME"

1. Use a Bible with a readable translation. There are many translations which are effective. The key is finding one which you understand.
2. Set a regular time and place. Determine when and where you can have the best uninterrupted time with God. For me, early morning works best. The key is, once the time and place is set, continue to make every effort at not allowing anything to disrupt your efforts to spend this valuable time with God.

3. *Ask God to reveal Himself to you and grant you wisdom from above.* James 1:5 says, "If any of you lacks wisdom, he should ask God, who gives generously to all..." Before beginning your time with God, take a time to realize you are in God's presence, and ask Him for wisdom to understand the Scripture you are about to read. Claim this promise and ask, "Lord, what do you want me to learn today? Teach me what you want me to know from your Word."

4. *Have a plan in mind.* Haphazard reading develops haphazard results. There are a number of devotional guides which are extremely effective including Walk through the Bible, Daily Bread, Growing Strong in the Seasons of Life, Cross Training Plan, Campus Journal, Drawing Near, etc. A good selection of Old and New Testament passages is recommended.

5. *Use your pen, and mark up your Bible.* Underline special passages, and make notes in your Bible. Ask, "How does this Scripture apply to me? How can I put this into practice today?" Keep a notebook with Quiet Time notes of lessons which God is teaching you, and incorporate this into your journal time (more on "Journaling" below).

6. *Maintain a regular journal.* A journal is much more than a diary of events summarizing the day. Here you can record specific items that you are learning and what God is teaching you through these experiences. I have kept a journal since I was seventeen. Spiritual growth and maturity are documented as the Lord has worked in my life.

7. *Make prayer a major part of your "Quiet Time."* I use a number of different methods including the ACTS method noted above. Another way of handling the prayer for others and yourself is to group certain people or things into certain days. For example, Sundays you may want to pray for your church and pastor; Mondays for national and local government; Tuesdays for family members; Wednesdays for coworkers or school mates; etc.

Perhaps you have had a regular "Quiet Time" in the past but it has grown old and/or ineffective. Here are some miscellaneous thoughts and suggestions to help invigorate.

1. *Read for inspiration.* It is not necessarily designed to be an in-depth study of a passage or book. It is meant to be an inspiration in your walk with Christ for that particular day.
2. *Don't take copious notes.* Save this for specific study sessions. Try to record one or two insights or promises that God gives you daily. You will soon have a bundle of precious jewels from God. These can be valuable in times of need and spiritual dryness.
3. *Have variety.* It is not necessary to do it exactly the same way every day. Have a plan, but feel free to vary.
4. *Be consistent.* Some days you may not feel like having a "Quiet Time." Do your best to even have just a short one, even if it is just reviewing underlined passages that God impressed on you in weeks and months before.
5. *Read with your mind open to God.* He will surprise you with insights and keen ideas and lead you to do some things you never thought you could or would do. Just give Him a chance.
6. *Expect a blessing.* You will receive this blessing if it is not just a legalistic ritual, but a personal, intimate fellowship with Almighty God. God desires our fellowship; He longs for it. And He will honor our willingness to spend time with Him.
7. *Pray before you read.* Ask God to give you wisdom and concentration in your reading. Then read and pray through the Scripture.
8. *Get it on your schedule.* If your regular time is early in the morning, then be committed to it. Satan would love to squeeze it out in the midst of numerous other activities. When you do blow it, confess it, forget it and renew your commitment to get back on track the next day.
9. *Make notes about passages or topics you want to study more at a later date.* Then go back to these lists and do it!

10. Meditate on what you read. A good way to keep in mind what you read is to check up on yourself throughout the day. I often ask myself, "What did I read in my Quiet Time today?" If you have difficulty recalling it, then you are not retaining any of it.

11. Remember the importance of spiritual food. Through the nourishing of our souls, we literally "eat God's Word." Our spiritual strength is directly related to our intake.

12. Enjoy it. Our "Quiet Time" should not be legalistic or drudgery.

FROM A FRIEND

Dear Friend,

How are you? I just had to send a note to tell you how much I care about you.

I saw you yesterday as you were talking with your friends. I waited all day, hoping you would want to talk with me, too. I gave you a sunset to close your day and a cool breeze to rest you—but I still love you because I am your friend.

I saw you sleeping last night and longed to touch your brow so I spilled moonlight upon your face. Again I waited, wanting to rush down so we could talk. I have so many gifts for you! You awoke and rushed off to work. My tears were in the rain.

If you would only listen to me! I love you! I try to tell you in blue skies and in the quiet, green grass. I whisper it in leaves on the trees and breathe it in colors of flowers, shout it to you in mountain streams, give the birds love songs to sing. I clothe you with warm sunshine and perfume the air with nature scents. My love for you is deeper than the ocean and bigger than the biggest need in your heart!

Ask me! Talk with me! Please don't forget me. I have so much to share with you! I won't hassle you any further. It is your decision. I have chosen you and I will wait—because I love you.

Your Friend,
Jesus

9

Sexual Temptations and Lust

Have you had any flirtatious or lustful attitudes, tempting thoughts, or exposed yourself to any explicit materials which would not glorify God?

Why does this area continue to be such a problem for men? Unfortunately, many reported incidents have been covered by local and national media involving people of faith who have fallen in this area of sexual temptation. It is not surprising that God's Word deals directly with this issue and the perils involved when not relying on Christ's power and His promises. Within the context of accountability this is one area which needs to be continually addressed by all accountability groups. WHY? Because it can jump up and attack you at anytime. It is one of Satan's strongest and effective tools.

Jerry Kirk says, "Choosing to let Jesus be Lord of your sex life will shape every other area of your life, because sexuality is at the center of our being. This decision will influence your current and future ability as a husband, father and Christian. Choosing purity is difficult, but for those who put in the hard work and prayer, living by Christ's standard is a road to deep joy and real sexual satisfaction." He adds, "This matters to God because it goes to the very heart of our witness, our understanding of God's faithfulness and the vital issue of whether we really believe God when He tells us a given course of action is better for us. It matters to God because He deeply loves us and wants us to enjoy that which is most fulfilling and meaningful. Practicing sexual purity, even though it's hard, is also one of the most accurate reflections of the depth of our relationship with Christ."[1]

WHAT DOES SCRIPTURE SAY?

"But I tell you that anyone who looks at a woman lustfully has already committed adultery with her in his heart." (Matthew 5:28)

"Rather, clothe yourselves with the Lord Jesus Christ, and do not think about how to gratify the desires of the sinful nature." (Romans 13:14)

"Do not love the world or anything in the world. If anyone loves the world, the love of the Father is not in him. For everything in the world—the cravings of sinful man, the lust of his eyes and the boasting of what he has and does—comes not from the Father but from the world. The world and its desires pass away, but the man who does the will of God lives forever." (1 John 2:15-17)

"But each one is tempted when, by his own evil desire, he is dragged away and enticed. Then, after desire has conceived, it gives birth to sin; and sin, when it is full-grown, gives birth to death." (James 1:14-15)

"Flee from sexual immorality. All other sins a man commits are outside his body, but he who sins sexually sins against his own body." (1 Corinthians 6:18)

"Flee the evil desires of youth, and pursue righteousness, faith love and peace, along with those who call on the Lord out of a pure heart." (2 Timothy 2:22)

"Because he himself suffered when he was tempted, he is able to help those who are being tempted." (Hebrews 2:18)

"No temptation has seized you except what is common to man. And God is faithful; he will not let you be tempted beyond what you can bear. But when you are tempted, he will also provide a way out so that you can stand up under it." (1 Corinthians 10:13)

"Finally, brothers, whatever is true, whatever is noble, whatever is right, whatever is pure, whatever is lovely, whatever is admirable—if anything is excellent or praiseworthy—think about such things." (Philippians 4:8)

Scripture tells us that Jesus has encountered every temptation, yet without sin (Hebrews 4:15-16), so it is an encouragement to know we can approach him with confidence to help us in our time of need.

WHAT ARE PEOPLE SAYING?

Every time I talk about our accountability questions, this particular question frequently gets the same reaction from men. One common response has been, "This is an area I really need to talk about." In fact, in passing along these questions to hundreds of men, I have only met one person who said he had no problems or temptations with lust—I didn't believe him.

In my own life I battled these temptations for years. Because of my position as a Christian leader, I did not feel I could confess this to anyone. I thought it would damage my relationships with those around me, so I silently hid them. Though I remained a virgin until I married, I had been exposed to inappropriate materials (via television, magazines and books) as well as my own desires of the flesh. My mind was stained with pictures which I had difficulty removing from my past. I would be victorious for a season or two, but then during times of loneliness or despair, Satan would strike quickly, and the garbage would return. Because I believe that God judges our thought life equally with the actual act, I knew my sin as well as God did (Matthew 5:28).

Imagine my surprise when I joined the accountability group and found men who began to verbalize the temptations of lust that they were also battling with, and I discovered that I was not alone. Up to that point in time I thought I was the only one who battled these issues. I also began to share my sin and soon found that I was able to release for the first time in my life, some of the garbage that had consumed my life. We encouraged one another to remove the junk. Incredible freedom began to occur and Christ became alive in my life in this area, enabling me and others to see positive, victorious results for the first time.

Rather than continually being overwhelmed by the lack of success, we began telling stories of how we had remained pure, unstained when faced with areas where we had historically stumbled. Even today, it is exciting to see how we can rejoice to see men standing strong. Having been married for the past two and half years, I can honestly say that my accountability group helped me to recover from the past and prepared me to be the kind of spouse who would be completely faithful to my wife. However, I do know that being married does not necessarily make it easier to overcome lustful temptations than when I was single. In fact, I am bombarded continually in my marriage by all types of temptations. I know that Satan's attacks have only become stronger since he loves to throw destruction in my path hoping I too will fall, as so many others have done in the past.

Forgiveness Is Available

If you have fallen in the past, today you can start anew and begin the journey of seeking God and His will. Jesus Christ's shed blood provides forgiveness and will put you back on a life of purity. Scripture reminds us that complete forgiveness is available.

Titus 3:3-5 says, "At one time we too were foolish, disobedient, deceived and enslaved by all kinds of passions and pleasures. We lived in malice and envy, being hated and hating one another. But when the kindness and love of God our Savior appeared, he saved us, not because of righteous things we had done, but because of his mercy. He saved us through the washing of rebirth and renewal by the Holy Spirit. 1 John 1:9 reports, "If we confess our sins, he is faithful and just and will forgive us our sins and purify us from all unrighteousness." Philippians 3:12-14 reminds us of Paul's outlook, "Not that I have already obtained all this, or have already been made perfect, but I press on to take hold of that for which Christ Jesus took hold of me. Brothers, I do not consider myself yet to have taken hold of it. But one thing I do: Forgetting what is behind and straining toward what is ahead, I press on toward the goal to win the prize for which God has called me heavenward in Christ Jesus."

Let's be honest! Sexual purity is not easy, whether you're a seasoned believer or a new follower of Christ. I want to encourage each of you to remain pure at all costs. God commands us to live upright and pure, saving ourselves for marriage. With the strength of the Almighty God and the help of people around you, you can do it. Let me share with you some ways that you can minimize sexual temptations.

TELEVISION

What we see on television today is absolutely disgusting. We see all the flesh we want, not only on cable channels such as HBO, Showtime, Cinemax (I call it "Sin to the Max"), Playboy, MTV, etc. but also regular network stations, too. Every person who desires purity ought to evaluate every single station and program to determine whether or not it is appropriate viewing material.

I would also encourage you not to "channel surf" by using your remote to flip through the channels continually. No matter how innocent it is, you will eventually get to a channel that you should not be watching, and it is difficult to keep the remote going when a sexy scene is unfolding before you. Though we have cable in our home, we have made decisions about what we are going to watch, and we do not stray from these. An easy guideline in evaluating what is inappropriate viewing is to ask the following question: "How would Jesus, your spouse or children react to this particular show?" There was a period of time during my single years when I placed a picture of Christ directly above my television set. That really helped keep me on track!

When traveling away from home and in a hotel, here are several suggestions to help remain on the straight and narrow:

1. Take pictures of your family, children, spouse or girlfriend, and place them all around the television set.
2. Before checking into your room, ask the hotel to turn off the premium channels on your set.
3. Specifically ask one of your accountability partners to quiz you on the amount of television and the specific shows you watched while away from home.
4. Do not even turn on the set. Instead, spend concentrated time studying Scripture and praying.
5. Whenever possible, arrange to stay with friends either in your hotel room or in their home.

Find a church. Mid week services?

MOVIES

Call the E-Team

Once again, evaluate beforehand the movies you will be watching by reviewing the rating, using common sense and listening to the comments of people you trust. And if something becomes steamy, feel free to leave the theater entirely or at least leave to go get some popcorn.

MAGAZINE RACKS

Believe me, after being in hundreds of airports, gas stations and grocery stores, these magazines always have a way of catching your eye. My advice is to just turn and walk away. This is one more tool of Satan to lure you into sexual temptation.

THE BEACH/PARK/MALL OR VIRTUALLY ANYWHERE

There is nothing I can do about the first look, but the second-third-fourth look I can control. Appreciate God's handiwork, but do not take the additional looks. When you do, you could be treading on dangerous ground. No matter where you go, you are bound to see someone who is attractive. Be aware that the additional looks are where trouble begins. If you have to, just drop your head or deliberately focus on something else until he or she passes by.

SOME THOUGHTS FOR SINGLES

I was extremely pleased with the response that the "True Love Waits" campaign received across America in 1994. Over 400,000 teens pledged to remain sexually pure until marriage. What a wonderful statement. When I was growing up, you were not cool if you were a virgin. I am glad to see that so many have decided to remove themselves from safe sex techniques and return to what the Bible says about sex: Wait until you are married.

When I got I married, I was 32 years old, and I admit it was not easy to remain pure, but I did it! At times while dating, my conduct was not at a level which pleased God or myself, but He protected me in a powerful way. Know your boundaries before you get yourself in a bad situation. Part of this can be controlled through your surroundings such as not going back to your apartment after dinner, knowing your roommates will not be there. This is extremely tempting. Some good guidelines from a family I know are: (1) no touching below the chin or above the elbow, (2) never lie down beside someone and (3) no extended kissing. Believe me, going beyond these three things can and will lead to compromise.

What About If You're Married?

Many couples vow to God, their family and friends on their wedding day their complete commitment to one another. Yet, so often we see unfaithfulness to the partners by entering into inappropriate relations with people from the opposite sex. The surveys tell us that over a third of all men cheat on their spouses. The Bible clearly tells us this is wrong.

Living a Life of Sexual Purity

God has set a high standard, albeit one that will bless us and those we love. Here are some key principles many men have found helpful:

1. *Past mistakes don't mean future failure!* Few if any Christian men are without some sexual sin. But a mistake in the past is no reason to give up practicing sexual purity. Confession and forgiveness can cleanse.
2. *Sexual purity is as much a matter of the mind as it is of the body.* Romans 12:1-2 refers to "being transformed by the renewing of your mind." Allowing sinful thoughts to take root in our minds and hearts is the first sign of an actual physical sex sin. Nourishing thoughts of sexual unfaithfulness will later be difficult to resist.
3. *Practicing sexual purity is a process as well as a commitment.* This must be cultivated like any other godly habit, or it will not be there when temptation comes. Joseph fled without his cloak rather than sin against God with Potiphar's wife (see Genesis 39).

4. *Don't pretend your desires don't exist.* Denial doesn't work. God created us as sexual beings, and our desires are normal. We need to channel them in productive, God-given directions.

5. *No substitute exists for personal accountability with other godly men.* Secret sins have much more power and usually last much longer than those we acknowledge to our brothers.

6. *Understand the importance of sexual purity to our marriages, families and heritage.* Our faithfulness gives strength to our wives and children.

7. *Understand the importance of sexual purity to our Christian witness.* Nothing undermines our influence more than sexual failure. We must work on purity not only for our own well-being and joy but also for the health of the church.

8. *Understand the importance of sexual purity to our own sexual fulfillment within marriage.* In God's design we become one spiritually and emotionally when we become "one flesh." Thus, a man brings to his marriage bed every woman with whom he has ever had intercourse. Each can affect his ability to wholeheartedly and single-mindedly love his wife and enjoy true and unique intimacy with her. Men who have premarital sexual encounters will regret it.[2]

HOW TO AVOID SEXUAL TEMPTATION
by John Maxwell
(Presented at 1994 Promise Keeper's Conference)

1. Run!!
2. Accept responsibility for your failures.
3. Be accountable.
4. Listen to your wife.
5. Be on your guard. Some safeguards include:
   *Don't travel alone (if possible).
   *Call your wife nightly (when traveling).
   *Don't be alone with a woman.
   *Talk positively about your wife.

*Carefully pick your close friends.

6. Determine to live a pure life.
7. Realize that sexual sin prostitutes Christ's Lordship.
8. Recognize the consequences of sexual sin.
9. Think about your children.
10. Get a new definition of success.

[1] Jerry Kirk, *Seven Promises of a Promise Keeper* (Colorado Springs, CO: Focus on the Family, 1994), pp. 92-93.
[2] Adapted from Jerry Kirk, *Seven Promises of a Promise Keeper* (Colorado Springs, CO: Focus on the Family, 1994), pp. 94-97.

10

Financial Dealings

Have you been completely above reproach in your financial dealings?

During my college years at Central Washington University I earned a degree in accounting and later received my Certified Public Accountant's license while working for Ernst & Whinney, a public accounting firm. However, what I want to tell you in the following section has little to do with what I learned in the education system. It has much more to do with the application of Biblical principles and common sense.

What Does Scripture Say?

All money belongs to God and we are simply caretakers of it for a short period of time (Matthew 24:45-51 and Luke 16:10-13). As a steward of these funds, we are responsible for properly managing this property while we have it in our possession. God can decide to entrust us with as much or as little as He chooses. If we are faithful in our stewardship, God makes certain promises to us including peace (John 14:27), provision (Matthew 6:31-33) and prosperity (Matthew 19:29).

Also, anything of material value which takes priority over God and carries with it symptoms of worry, greed, resentment, self indulgence, poor record-keeping, anger and DEBT creates "financial bondage." This usually occurs for three reasons:

1. *Financial ignorance:* There is a vast number of people in the world today who are not aware of financial matters or the responsibilities associated therewith, nor are they interested in understanding numbers (Proverbs 24:3-4).
2. *Wrong attitudes:* Greed is a primary reason (James 3:16).
3. *Poor planning:* This includes a lack of budget preparation, using debt financing and not properly utilizing advisors around you (Proverbs 16:9).

Anyone can improve and enhance their financial situation by applying the following principles.

TITHING

The Bible clearly instructs us to tithe to the church and God's work here on earth. There are many opinions as to what the correct percentage should be. Because I believe that God owns everything, the pressure to determine a set percentage is relieved. As a suggestion, a minimum 10% of your gross (pre-tax) wages should be a starting point. Freely give, and you will discover the joy of participating in God's grace in ways you never dreamed possible. In our own personal finances we have discovered that giving above and beyond 10% of our income has been a great blessing and joy. If you want to be free from financial bondage, this is the first area I would address (Malachi 3:8).

Frankly, it was discouraging for me as a CPA to prepare income tax returns several years ago for my Christian friends and to discover that they were giving practically nothing to their church and charities. One couple was making in excess of $50,000 and very vocal about their Christian faith and church involvement, yet had given less than $50 annually. I confronted them on their lack of giving, and they told me that they were too poor to give and had nothing to spare. In later years as their income mounted, they were in financial bondage because I believe God's blessing was not on their life primarily due to their stance on tithing. This couple had difficulty accepting the fact that all money belongs to God.

On the flip side, I have seen people give who had literally nothing and watched God bless them financially because their priorities were in order.

ELIMINATE DEBT

The Bible is specific about debt, that it is not a normal situation, yet it is permitted in certain cases (Psalms 37:21). We are also not to accumulate long-term debt, to avoid surety (which is borrowing without the ability to repay), to make an absolute commitment to repay everything we do owe (Ecclesiastes 5:5) and while in debt realize that you are not as flexible because a debtor is in servitude to the lender (Proverbs 22:7). The only debt I am comfortable with is for home financing, yet even with this debt I encourage you to pay off the balance as quickly as possible. For example, if you make one additional full payment on a 30-year mortgage every year, you will completely repay the entire debt in about 19 years.

Outside of home financing, I believe you should not have any other debt. I realize this may sound unorthodox. However, no matter how persuasive the arguments to borrow may be, it just works out better not to become the borrower to anyone whether it pertains to car loans, student loans or any other type of loan.

If you are currently facing large debts, then begin the process immediately of ridding yourself of this burden by making the needed payments to remove the debt completely.

If this is not possible, then seek counsel and begin to develop a pay back plan. One of the members of our group became debt-free this past year, primarily because the group helped him develop a plan to do so.

Credit Cards

For some it may be wiser to completely eliminate all credit card activity. I know some who have elected this alternative, primarily because of a bad credit experience or an inability to monitor such activity. If you do need a card, my advice is simple. Find one credit card which meets your needs and get rid of all others. Then make a commitment to repay the entire balance every single month. By making minimum payments, you will suffer from extraordinary interest charges in just a short period of time. This is unwise (Proverbs 20:16).

If possible, look for a card which will benefit you. For instance, some will give you frequent-flier miles, credits toward major purchases such as cars or refrigerators or even cash rebates.

Distinguish Needs Versus Wants

Evaluate every single purchase you make by two categories. Virtually every "want" is not necessary if you take the time to consider why you desire it. And with needs, do your homework. I am a stickler for finding sales or bargains, and many times I will hold off purchasing something initially until I find it on sale. Sometimes neighborhood garage sales offer many of the items on the need list. Also, do not forget to use coupons. I enjoy looking for this source of free money which is available to us everyday through the mail, newspapers and books.

BUDGETING

Though I realize this can be a painful process, I encourage you to keep close track of all your incoming and outgoing funds through the use of a budget plan. Initially, maintain records of all funds spent, including cash over a three to six month basis, to determine average spending levels. Then set maximum spending levels on a variety of matters. Include in your plan items such as tithe, savings and investments as well as your housing, utilities, food, recreation, emergency car and/or house repairs, etc. Once your plan is set, stick to it. This is extremely important for everyone but particularly for families. Commit your plan to prayer, and ask God to give you wisdom and direction (Proverbs 16:3).

GOOD RECORD-KEEPING

No matter how unorganized you claim to be, there is no excuse for sloppy financial record-keeping. Reconcile your checkbook on a timely basis, keep your files of financial records up-to-date, keep your will and beneficiary information current, maintain all prior year income tax information and other key financial data in a safe, secure place. As a steward of what God has given you, you have a great responsibility to keep track of it.

RENDER UNTO CAESAR WHAT IS CAESAR'S

Have honesty and integrity in dealing with all your taxes and bills (Matthew 22:17-21). Completely repay all your debts in their entirety, and do not cheat on your taxes.

Here is an example that I related to my group last year. We were preparing to sell our house when I discovered a termite problem. When the exterminator showed up, I was told I could spend $130 to partially fix the problem in order to meet the minimum standards for selling the house or spend $500 and be sure the problem was resolved. It crossed my mind to go for the lower option, but I did not feel it would be honest. Therefore, I went for the $500 job, much to his surprise. Upon completion of the work, I was told that my response was rare, and he was curious what I did for a living. It gave me a great opportunity to tell him about my work with the FCA and my faith in Christ. Later that night we got a full price offer on our home. I am confident that because we did the right thing, God blessed us. God desires for us to be upright in all our financial dealings.

Identify Scams and Get Rich Schemes

We have made it our policy to not buy or commit to anything over the telephone. I cannot tell you how many times we have been called by a variety of people wanting our money for some worthy cause or on how we can get-rich-quick. Our response is always for people to send us information in the mail, and we will be glad to review and read their material for ourselves. Most of the time, the materials are never sent and usually, if they are received, you can discover the small print very quickly. If I have questions that I cannot answer, I have the freedom to take these materials to outsiders that I trust for valuable counsel.

At other times, you will be approached in person by people who will make strong sales calls, and you will feel unable to say "NO." I urge you to not feel compelled to agree to something until you are totally sure. I have walked away from many opportunities until I have had a chance to review and pray through situations using the wisdom of my wife, my family and friends to help me determine the right course of action. The times I have acted alone and have reacted quickly, primarily out of greed, are when I have been burned financially.

DIVERSIFYING YOUR ASSETS

In current economic times it is important that your eggs are not all in one basket. Spread out your funds into several different banks and institutions and possibly across national boundaries. Obtain a combination of cash and other high liquid accounts to go alongside other investment options such as stocks, bonds, real estate, insurance contracts, etc. I also would get several trustworthy investment advisors who can help you manage your funds appropriately and minimize your overall risk.

SAVING FOR THE FUTURE

It is very important that you have funds ready to meet your future needs and those of your family. Set aside a portion of your monthly income to help you meet your medium and long-range financial goals. This includes the needs you have for life insurance, retirement and children's college education fund. I also believe you should have a cash disaster fund to help offset major unexpected bills such as car repairs, medical expenses, etc.

FAMILY FINANCES

It is sad to report that today's church families are some of the most negligent when it comes to financial issues. Larry Burkett reports the following for "church families" from his seminar, "Your Finances in Changing Times":

* 40% are overspending every month.
* 20% are on the verge of divorce.
* 50% of all these marriages end in divorce.
* 90% of the divorces point to financial difficulties.

One of Satan's primary methods for destroying families is through financial matters. 1 Timothy 6:10, 11, 17 says, "For the love of money is a root of all kinds of evil. Some people, eager for money, have wandered from the faith and pierced themselves with many griefs. But you, man of God, flee from all this, and pursue righteousness, godliness, faith, love, endurance and gentleness. Command those who are rich in this present world not to be arrogant nor to put their hope in wealth, which is so uncertain, but to put their hope in God, who richly provides us with everything for our enjoyment."

Keep your lives free from the love of money, and be content with what you have because God has said in Hebrews 13:5, "Never will I leave you; never will I forsake you."

Matthew 6:19-21 says, "Do not store up for yourselves treasures on earth, where moth and rust destroy, and where thieves break in and steal. But store up for yourselves treasures in heaven, where moth and rust do not destroy, and where thieves do not break in and steal. For where your treasure is, there your heart will be also."

It is crucial within a marriage to decide who will handle paying the bills, balancing the checkbook, doing the research and making the investment decisions. Once this is decided, it is important that both have input and full knowledge about financial matters. Periodically, take an inventory of everything that relates to money (savings and checking accounts; credit-cards; life, health and auto insurance policies; stocks, bonds, mutual funds and other investments; and real estate holdings) so there are no surprises for either of you. Also, make sure you have a valid will and that your estate planning is in order in case of an untimely death.

As the Scriptures state so clearly, there are great dangers associated with the accumulation of riches and how they impact our lives and those around us. I believe the key is to: *surrender total control to God.* Only when you allow God to be in total control of this area will you experience peace in your financial matters.

28 MONEY-SAVING TIPS

1. Have a specific and realistic savings goal, in writing, with deadline dates. Even saving small amounts can add up to large sums of money over time.
2. Keep track of all your expenses (including cash), and review them at the end of each month so you know where your money is going.
3. Learn the difference between wants and needs. Focus your spending on the needs.
4. Build an emergency fund equal to three to six months' living expenses or more if you can, and keep it in a safe and liquid investment.
5. Insure yourself and your loved ones adequately against loss of property, job or income and against legal liability and major medical expenses.
6. Pay off all your credit card debt every month. You should never make an interest payment on your credit card. Look for a "no-fee" card or one that has incentives for airline, automobile or cash credits.
7. Do not buy or rent more house than you can afford. Do not let your mortgage or rent make it impossible for you to save.
8. If you have a mortgage and have no other higher-interest debt, pay the mortgage off as quickly as you can by making extra payments toward the principal.
9. Look for quality and comfort, not excessive display, in your home's furnishings.
10. Drop expensive "add-on" services you can easily do without such as extra features on your telephone or cable television.
11. Take full advantage of coupon and refund offers, but do not buy anything you do not need just because you have a coupon or will get a rebate.
12. Shop the grocery stores and wholesale clubs that save you the most money and time.

13. Look at your car only as a contraption to take you from point A to point B, not as a status symbol.
14. Buy sufficient liability coverage for your car, but refuse to pay for excessive collision or comprehensive insurance.
15. Buy the best quality clothes you can find at reasonable prices, and take care of them so they will last a long time. Also, color-coordinate your wardrobe to save on shoes and other accessories.
16. Do not buy something which will require two incomes to pay for.
17. Learn to see, read and listen to ads and to extract the useful information from among all the hype.
18. Do not shop on impulse or because you are bored, but make a list of the things you need and stick to it. Do not feel obligated to buy everything on your list immediately, but take time to research.
19. Learn to enjoy life's simple pleasures, many of which are free.
20. Shop around for the best deal among banks and savings and loans, and refuse to keep your money in low-interest, high-fee bank checking accounts.
21. Learn about mutual funds, and then use them to diversify your investments.
22. Educate yourself about taxes and tax rates. The Internal Revenue Service will answer your questions (1-800-829-1040) and send you dozens of publications for free (1-800-829-3676).
23. Estimate at the beginning of each year how much your income from all sources is going to be, then adjust your withholding at work so you come as close to a zero refund or payment at tax preparation time.
24. Contribute the maximum allowed to your employer's 401(k) salary deferral plan and to your Individual Retirement Account or a tax-sheltered annuity vehicle. Look for employer matching fund incentives.

25. Educate yourself about investing. With so many excellent magazines and books available, there is no excuse not to do so. Invest wisely with investments that will let you sleep at night. Greed will lead to destruction.
26. Take care of yourself. Keep in good health so you can enjoy the fruits of all your labor and savings and share that enjoyment with your loved ones.
27. Share a portion of your fortune with your local church and favorite charity. Feel the joy of helping others less fortunate than yourself.
28. Make sure your will and estate planning issues are in proper order.

List compiled by Rod Handley

11

Quality Relationships

Have you spent quality relationship time with family and friends?

God has charged men with providing leadership in their homes and families. Leadership in the form of loving authority, leadership in the form of spiritual training and leadership in maintaining the marital relationship. As part of this role, developing and maintaining quality relationships is so important. The Bible urges us to embrace one another's pains and triumphs.

When I was single, the subject of "quality time" came up every now and then. Frankly, I had no clue what it meant. My accountability partners and my wife have helped me to begin to understand. It is not just spending time together, but time when you focus your attention on the one you are with, whether it be your spouse, child or friend. It is extremely rude to be in the midst of a conversation and have your attention diverted by things happening around you.

I am trying to put myself in the position of those whom I'm talking to during conversations. After all, if I am talking to someone, it is annoying to have people casually listening. Therefore, I have tried to implement the following when talking to people:

1. *Eye contact.* Get your focus off of the newspaper, TV and others nearby and make deliberate effort to truly hear them.
2. *Ask lots of questions, if appropriate.* There are times when you will need to be quiet and just listen, but many times you can help carry the flow of the conversation by knowing how and when to ask questions.
3. *Avoid clock watching.* If you have another appointment or things to do, let the person know up front what time constraints you have. If you have unlimited time, then remove your watch so complete attention can be given.
4. *Mix in your experiences, if appropriate.* Do not dominate the conversation but find a way to add your own thoughts without disrupting the flow of the conversation.

There are many people I would love to contact regularly, but with limited time I have had to make relationship priorities. Specifically determine how you intend to spend time with people around you. And in your relationship world, love without expectations in the same manner that God has demonstrated love to each one of us.

WHAT DOES SCRIPTURE SAY?

"A new command I give you: Love one another. As I have loved you, so you must love one another. By this all men will know that you are my disciples, if you love one another." (John 13:34-35)

"My command is this: Love each other as I have loved you. Greater love has no one than this, that he lay down his life for his friends." (John 15:12-13)

"Let us therefore make every effort to do what leads to peace and to mutual edification." (Romans 14:19)

"Therefore encourage one another and build each other up, just as in fact you are doing." (1 Thessalonians 5:11)

GOD

In the midst of maintaining quality relationships, again, spending daily time with the Almighty God is the most important. See Chapter 8 on maintaining this as a key part of your day and life. Your other friendships will be enhanced when this is your top priority.

SPOUSE

After God, your spouse is the next most important relationship which you have. Usually during courtship it is easy to focus your energies on your future mate, but many stop the romance within hours of saying, "I do." To maintain a successful marriage, it is important to continue the dating process. This means setting aside specific date nights just for the two of you to get away and enjoy each other's company. This becomes even more critical when you have children. Recently, Janna and I escaped for an entire weekend by ourselves, and it was a wonderful getaway experience.

Another great habit is to spend time praying together on a regular basis. Be specific in your requests and open about your needs and concerns. As spouses, we are called to love, respect and submit to one another. Each of us also has specific needs. For women, this includes care, understanding, respect, devotion, validation and reassurance. Men need trust, acceptance, appreciation, admiration, approval and encouragement.

Gary Smalley has many solid messages to give to couples. His "five secrets of a happy marriage" are:

1. *Healthy couples have a clearly defined menu of expectations.* They have made certain decisions relating to how they are going to interact together (i.e. how they will honor one another, a plan for dealing with unresolved anger, activities that foster emotional bonding, etc.).

2. *Healthy couples understand and practice meaningful communication.* The goal is to feel safe in sharing honestly and intimately with one another.
3. *Healthy couples are associated with a small, healthy support group.* Regular time with three or four couples can make an incredible difference in your own marriage.
4. *Healthy couples are aware of unhealthy or offensive behavior stemming from their heritage.* Make a conscious decision to overcome past mistakes and look to gain support for the changes.
5. *Healthy couples have a vibrant relationship with Jesus Christ.* Be totally dependent upon Him as our primary source of abundant life. Your spouse will let you down at some point—Christ doesn't.[1]

There are so many resources and ideas available in enhancing your relationship with your spouse. Here are 10 brief tips which might help you in making a decision about getting married or in reinforcing some of the basic principles involved in every successful marriage.

1. *Lifelong Commitment.* When a man and a woman decide to marry, they are committing themselves to remain together forever, until death. "What God has joined together, let man not separate." (Matthew 19:6)
2. *Shared Identity.* In marriage a man and woman are brought into union—"they will become one flesh" (Genesis 2:24). They become one as they blend their lives together. It's once-for-all, yet it's a process that needs time, love, patience and forgiveness (Genesis 2:23-24).
3. *Absolute Faithfulness.* Marital faithfulness is the fulfillment of the vow made before God during the wedding ceremony. The Bible demands sexual fidelity. "You shall not commit adultery." (Exodus 20:14).

4. *Unreserved Love.* This is genuine, heartfelt, through-thick-and-thin, till-death-do-us-part love. A husband and a wife are to love each other with an unreserved love that leads them to honor one another, to esteem one another, to consider one another's welfare above their own and to stay by one another's side through the highs and lows of marriage. "Love never fails." (1 Corinthians 13:8)

5. *Mutual Submission.* Submission and love go together. We know that God is love, but how do we know He loves us? Because with great humility and submission, Christ went to the cross (Philippians 2:5-8). Marriage is give and take. It is overcoming selfishness. It is being a servant.

6. *Well-defined Roles.* Marriage works best when both husband and wife accept their roles. It's a functional necessity exemplified by Jesus. He came to earth to carry out the will and plan of God. Although He was equal to the Father, He submitted to the Father's leading. When the Bible says that the husband is the head of the wife (Ephesians 5:23), it simply means that the husband is to provide responsible leadership without being dictorial or self-serving.

7. *Sexual Fulfillment.* Sexuality is not evil. Inside marriage it is not sinful. But it must not be made more important than it is, nor should it be minimized. It's part of the overall picture—an intimate part of the shared identity of husband and wife (1 Corinthians 7:3-4).

8. *Open Communication.* For a marriage to work, communication barriers must be broken down. These four suggestions might help:

(a) Tell of your need to communicate.
(b) Don't rehash old conversations.
(c) Start on the fact level.
(d) Move on to the feeling and conviction level.

9. *Tender Respect.* This is generally more a problem for men. Therefore, a husband must make it his goal to give his wife

special honor and respect, making sure he doesn't rob her of the joy of life.

10. Spiritual Companionship. What a difference it makes when a marriage has a godly husband a dedicated wife! Love and sacrifice will set this marriage apart and make possible a true spiritual companionship. As a man and wife draw closer to God, they will draw closer to each other.[2]

In closing, Dave Gibson, Associate Pastor of Grace Church in Edina, Minnesota, says there are twelve words which will save your marriage. "I am sorry. I was wrong. Please forgive me. I love you."

Children

Your kids also need concentrated time with you. No matter how old or young, this is a priority. Too often, children get our leftover time instead of the best. Jeff Kemp, Executive Director of Washington Family Council and former NFL quarterback says, "Children, our next generation, gain their sense of value, their identity and their character from the intimacy and quality of parental relationship."[3]

In a study during the 1970's a team of researchers wanted to learn how much time middle-class fathers spent playing and interacting with their small children. First, they asked a group of fathers to estimate the time spent with their one-year-old youngsters each day and received an average reply of fifteen to twenty minutes. To verify these claims, the investigators attached microphones to the shirts of small children for the purpose of recording actual parental verbalization. The results of the study were shocking. The average amount of time spent by these middle-class fathers with their small children was thirty-seven seconds per day! Their direct interaction was limited to 2.7 encounters daily, lasting ten to fifteen seconds each! That amount of time represented fatherhood for millions of America's children in the 1970's, and I believe the findings would be even more depressing today.[4]

Here are some timely tips from Walt Mueller to consider in helping your children respond positively to negative peer pressure:

1. *Teach your children about the powerful role that friends play in our lives.* An old proverb says, "He who walks with the wise grows wise, but a companion of fools suffers harm." Discuss examples of this principle that you see in the media and everyday life.
2. *Actively build your child's self-image from day one.* Kids who experience ignorance, absence, or cutting remarks from their parents are significantly more likely to go to their peers for the acceptance and approval that they so desperately need.
3. *Examine yourself.* A positive example is the greatest educational tool at a father's fingertips. Do *you* give in to negative peer pressure in your life?
4. *Encourage involvement in a positive peer group.* Positive peer pressure can be a powerful tool to help our kids make wise choices. There are church groups, scouts and other volunteer organizations where your children will be surrounded with others their age who are living responsibly and wisely, and learning how to reach out to others with compassion and sensitivity.
5. *Pray, pray, pray.* Ask God for wisdom, courage, and strength as you lead your children.[5]

PARENTS AND SIBLINGS

Whether you live in the same home, city or across the globe, this is also one relationship which needs specific attention. Maintaining communication, even when living far away, has to be a priority even if it is through the mail or by phone.

FRIENDS

As a single person, I used to dread my friends' weddings because it meant they would most likely drift totally out of my life. When Janna and I got married, we made a commitment to each other that we would continue to interact with friends from our single years. It has been positive for us to continue to make these relationships important.

I also encourage you to determine if your relationships are "draining" or "replenishing." By "draining" I am referring to those friends who are demanding in the effort to maintain (i.e., we give significantly more than we gain). On the flip side, "replenishing" relationships are when you are greatly encouraged and strengthened when spending time together. It is important to have a proportionate number of each, especially if you have a high number of "drainers" in your life.

PASTORS/MINISTERS/PRIESTS

Some of the most needy people may be those who are in full-time Christian service. Dr. Gary Oliver polled pastors and discovered that many are weary, wounded and discouraged. We may need to take an active part in replenishing and encouraging them. The statistics (among many others shared at the 1993 Promise Keepers conference in Boulder) show the following:

*90% are not trained.
*70% do not have a close friend.
*40% wanted to leave the ministry within the last three months.
*50% feel incapable of doing their job.
*37% have inappropriate sexual behavior.

Bill D. Hallstead, pastor of Church of Christ in Truman, Minnesota wrote an article titled, "Perils of the Professionally

Holy." In this piece he stated that a high number of pastors had failed sexually primarily due to three reasons:

1. *Over familiarity with God.* Many were so accustomed to the reality of God that they no longer stood in awe of Him. Because careers and all other aspects of life is wrapped around the church, pastors begin to lose the awe that keeps them in profound respect of the holy and righteous God who will judge His people.
2. *Sin saturation.* Pastors confront a numbing array of seeing peoples sins. Week after week, a torrent of sins needing forgiveness flows past them until they lose sense of the awfulness of sin. In dealing with so many gross sins, a pastor's temptation seems so minor. They preach forgiveness which also covers them as well as for those they minister to.
3. *Job overload.* Even our pastors need time away from God. After all, everyone else has a break from time to time. These times of break away should not violate the holiness of God, but instead keep the relationship with God fresh, new and exciting.

NEIGHBORS

We believe that God strategically places us in living situations where we are called to befriend those who live close by. This past Easter my wife and I made twelve loaves of homemade bread and delivered them to our neighbors. Block parties are so important. These provide a basis for building a community and letting your light shine to those you see regularly.

CO-WORKERS AND EMPLOYEES

This is a great place to develop tremendous friendships both in secular and Christian work places. Keep your eyes and ears open, and you will be blessed. When I was at Ernst & Whinney, I was surrounded by people who were extremely successful, as defined by the world's standards. Yet, as relationships were formed, I discovered they too had many significant needs and were receptive to sharing those with me. Don't let the appearance of "having it all together" stop you from developing relationships with those who you will spend time with on a regular basis.

Keeping Up With Those Who Live Far Away

Obviously, there are some people who live far enough away where it is not possible to see on a regular basis, and thus it becomes important to communicate either by letter or phone. Here are ways to keep in touch:

1. *Personal letters:* Mike Rohrbach taught me many years ago the value of writing at least one letter a day to someone as a source of encouragement. It is extremely uplifting to go my mailbox and find a note from someone, so for years I have made it my goal to write a letter every day to someone. I have also made a commitment that if anyone will write me, I will respond to them.
2. *Form letters:* If personal notes won't work, use a form letter to stay in touch with your address list, even these letters serve as an information source. Often, I will add a personal note or two even to a form letter to personalize it.
3. *Phone Calls:* Just like letters, I try to make one encouraging phone call a day to someone whom the Lord puts on my mind. Whether it be a local or long distance call, it is good to talk to someone everyday.

The goal of these instructions is to develop long, lasting friendships.

THE BUILDER AND THE WRECKER

I watched them tearing a building down,
A gang of men in a busy town.
With a yo heave ho and lusty yell
they swung a beam, a side wall fell.
I asked the foreman, "Are those men skilled,
the kind you would hire if you wanted to build?"
He laughed and said, "Why, no indeed,
just common labor is all I need.
They can easily wreck in a day or two
what builders have taken years to do."
So, I asked myself as I went my way,
which of those roles have I tried today?
Am I the builder who works with care,
measuring life by the rule and square,
patiently following a well-made plan
carefully doing the best I can?
Or am I the wrecker who walks the town,
content with the labor of tearing down?
Author Unknown

[1] Adapted from *Seven Promises of a Promise Keeper* by Gary Smalley (Colorado Springs, CO: Focus on the Family, 1994), pp. 107-113.
[2] Adapted from "What Will Make My Marriage Work?" by David Egner (Sports Spectrum Magazine, January/February 1992), p. 24.
[3] Washington Citizen, September 1994, p.2.
[4] James Dobson, *What Wives Wish Their Husbands Knew About Women* (Wheaton, IL: Tyndale, 1975), pp. 157-158.
[5] Today's Father, published by National Center for Fathering, Vol. 2, No. 3

12

Our 100% Best

Have you done your 100% best in your job, school, etc.?

In my job with FCA there are times when I am asked what kind of athlete would Jesus Christ be. My response has always been, "He would be the best, not only in terms of performance, but also in terms of His attitude and work ethic." With this in mind I believe we are also called to that same type of effort in whatever environment we are placed.

WHAT DOES SCRIPTURE SAY?

Colossians 3:17 instructs, "And whatever you do, whether in word or deed, do it all in the name of the Lord Jesus, giving thanks to God the Father through him." Colossians 3:23-24 adds, "Whatever you do, work at it with all your heart, as working for the Lord, not for men, since you know that you will receive an inheritance from the Lord as a reward. It is the Lord Christ you are serving."

God expects our best effort in all of our endeavors. Whether on the job, in the classroom, on the athletic field, within our church or with our spouse, children and family, we are supposed to do it to our fullest ability for God's glory. God is our audience, not our employer, teacher, coach, pastor or spouse. When we remember that He is the one whom we serve, our performance can be centered solely on Him.

According to 1 Thessalonians 4:11-12, "Make it your ambition to lead a quiet life, to mind your own business and to work with your hands, just as we told you, so that your daily life may win the respect of outsiders and so that you will not be dependent on anybody." 1 Corinthians 10:31 is the bottom line, "So whether you eat or drink or whatever you do, do it all for the glory of God." Both of these passages point to a strong work ethic and excellence in all matters.

A Football Illustration

When I was a high school senior, we had a great football team with a perfect 9-0 record and a #1 rating in the state. However, one of the greatest lessons and memories of that season was learned from a scrawny sophomore during an early season practice. Tim Tontz was a speedy 135-pounder who specialized in punt returns. On our senior-dominated squad he made a mark on our team.

At the end of each practice our coaches had the entire team do extra running drills to help us in our conditioning. As seniors we knew the routine and the effort needed to make it through this time. At best, we were giving a 75% effort but since we all went at the same pace, no one got in trouble. The problem was Tim. While the rest of the team coasted, Tim would sprint the entire distance. He consistently beat everyone by a wide margin. Because of Tim we ended up running more than we wanted.

As one of the leaders of our team and a friend of Tim's, I finally decided to approach him and explain that he was making us look bad. "Tim, slow down, and go our speed," I pleaded. His words back to me knocked me over: "Rod, I am disappointed in you as a fellow Christian. You see, when I play or practice, I picture Jesus Christ in the stands cheering me on to do my best. You and the other seniors can jog if you want; I am going to play for Him."

I learned a valuable lesson that day that I have never forgotten, and it changed my whole perspective on athletics. I pushed myself in those practices to stay up with Tim, and our whole team responded to his leadership. I know this contributed to our success. But the attitude carried on for me off the playing field. Jesus became my audience, and no longer do I perform for anyone but Him.

We all have been given unique talents and abilities which God wants us to use completely. In all you do, do it for Him, and allow Him to use you to the fullest. Many times I hear people distinguishing their work performance or various daily activities from other aspects of their life. Does this bring glory to God? Let me give you some specifics.

ON THE JOB

As employees, we are called to give our employer our best possible effort. Do you work diligently, or do you hang out at the coffee pot? Do you give a minimal effort, or do you strive for excellence? Do you try to keep learning, or have you stagnated? Do you maintain a positive spirit with your peers, or do you spend time gossiping and tearing down others? Do you complain and even become embittered about your salary situation, especially when you compare yourself to others in the organization? Do you think of others, or do you always think of yourself? Do you aspire to dream big to help the company? Do you accurately compute your travel expenses? Does Jesus Christ shine through you on your job?

In answering these questions can you stand before God and your employer and honestly say you have done your best? When I worked in Seattle for Ernst & Whinney, one of the national accounting firms, I answered to some very demanding people. As I became more aware that I was working for the Lord and not for them, I began to excel in the work place. I could have easily cut corners or been slightly dishonest or just done enough to get by. But does that please God?

Measure your performance against a standard of working for Jesus Christ. It takes having a teachable spirit and self-discipline. Successful professionals make the fine art of self-criticism as natural and frequent as handing out business cards. It takes hard work to develop a discipline of reflection and then put it to work.

In addition, Romans 13:1-7 reminds us also that all authority has been granted by God and that we are given no other options but to submit to that authority. These Scriptures also tell us that we will find favor with God if we willingly place ourselves under the authority.

All employees must guard against workaholism. In the rush to put in longer and longer hours, what often gets neglected is the personal side: family, friends, church, hobbies. Too much driving to achieve, succeed and control can lead to overreliance on the job for satisfaction. The key is finding a balance to lead a personal and professional life where both are equally gratifying.

I believe long hours at the office aren't necessarily wrong, but it is the attitude that often comes with it. Workaholics often feel safer in the office because they know their hard work and a tough attitude will lead to success and approval whereas the emotional relationships at home may be more tenuous. At the office the workaholic is a corporate hero by being available around the clock, demanding of self and others to succeed at all costs. Harder work yields more success and recognition. The imbalance begins to feed on itself. The final results are a domination of work on the individual's time and energy with neglected personal relationships.

If you are a workaholic or close to becoming one, I challenge you to evaluate the way you schedule your time and set priorities. Ask God for wisdom and direction. Talk to your spouse and your accountability partners on how to better balance your life. Learn to say "no" to after-hours work commitments when they conflict with personal life. Take real vacations and enjoy the benefits of a weekend away from work to not only relax but also restore yourself when you return to the job.

WHAT IF YOU ARE THE BOSS?

In supervising people are you fair? Do you set a Christian example for your co-workers? Do you encourage and bless those you work with? Do you empower others to do their best? When you are the boss, it is important to communicate and be sensitive to those who work with you. When situations are not working out right, you need to assist them in improving their performance, if possible, or help them get into an environment where they can succeed.

As a supervisor if you find yourself constantly out of time, buried in trivia, unable to get the important things done while helping everyone else; you're probably suffering from one of leadership's most common diseases: the failure to delegate and empower others. Moses faced the same problem. After leading his people out of Egypt, he insisted on ruling personally. His "micro-leadership" kept him so involved, in fact, that the Scriptures report that he was busy from morning until evening. Fortunately, Moses' father-in-law Jethro gave Moses some great advice in Exodus 18:18-27: "You and these people who come to you will only wear yourselves out. The work is too heavy for you; you cannot handle it alone...that will make your load lighter, because they will share it with you. If you do this and God so commands, you will be able to stand the strain, and all these people will go home satisfied." (v. 18, 22b, 23)

Jethro was right! No one person can do it all. Furthermore, there are probably people in your organization who can do certain jobs better than you. You must learn to delegate. Though some are reluctant to do so, there are far more reasons to delegate than to do everything yourself.

School

Grades are not necessarily an indication of your effort. Even in my days cheating on exams was commonplace. During my sophomore year of college I had a golden opportunity to cheat on a final. A buddy of mine had stolen the test and had it "aced." Though I needed a good grade, I just could not participate with him, so I spent many hours preparing for this exam while he lounged in the student center. On test day he finished the exam within 30 minutes while I labored for over two hours along with the rest of the class. Imagine our surprise when the final grades were posted that I got an A for the semester, while he settled for a B. Again the Lord gets the glory for this happening, and I learned another lesson.

My advice when it comes to schooling is to strive to be the best you can be by not missing classes, performing all your homework and truly making an attempt to learn the material, not just get your grade. Also, honor the Lord, and have Him be your audience.

Time Management

An area of great frustration for many people, especially as they relate to doing their best in their day-to-day life, is the issue of having limited time. If you are like me, I somehow believe that if we had 30-hour days or at least an extra five or ten hours each week, my problems would be solved. Surely this extra time would relieve the tremendous pressure. Unfortunately our lives leave a trail of unfinished tasks, unanswered letters, unvisited friends, unread books and neglected family relations. But would a longer day solve our problem? Wouldn't we soon be as frustrated as we are now with our 24-hour allotment?

Each of us is given the same 24 hours a day. How we use our time depends on our priorities and goals. We make the hours count for what we think is important. I am an advocate of working smart, not just long. At the end of life you have probably never heard someone say, "I wish I had spent more time at the office." Therefore, the important commodity called time requires attention to details and a specific plan of action, or your time can quickly begin to slip away. It is also crucial that you not become a workaholic or a loaf. Either label would be inappropriate for someone who claims to be "working for the Lord."

In his book,"Tyranny of the Urgent" Charles Hummel tells us about how Jesus Christ managed and controlled His time while He was on earth. Though He was God, He was also human, and He experienced many of the same pressures and strains of a shortage of time. Yet at the end of His brief three years of ministry, John 17:4 says, "I have brought you glory on earth by completing the work you gave me to do." With so many unmet physical and spiritual needs around Him, He had peace because He knew that He had finished the work God had given Him.

The key to Christ's success was that He got his daily instructions in quiet moments from the Father. Consistently, you see that nothing got in the way of His intimate time with God. If Jesus needed this time with God, how much more do you and I need to seek it out? Jesus, though His ministry could have easily extended another 5-50 years, knew God in a way where He experienced tremendous peace. Hummel says, "The path to freedom is continuing day by day to meditate on the Scriptures and gain our Lord's perspective."[1]

I strongly encourage you to read "Tyranny of the Urgent." It will give you great insights on how to distinguish between the important and urgent needs that come up daily. Here are some other time keys to consider in getting a handle of your time:

1. *Learn to delegate.* Find people who are skilled (or teach them) to perform the task. There are people who can perform as well. We tend to cling to the jobs we can do well. And when you give it away, acknowledge, praise and thank them for the final product.

2. *Control your time.* Do not let strong-willed people dominate your schedule. You are in charge of your time...if you are not, someone else will take advantage of it. Ephesians 5:15-17 says, "Be very careful, then, how you live—not as unwise but as wise, making the most of every opportunity, because the days are evil. Therefore do not be foolish, but understand what the Lord's will is."be careful how you walk, not as unwise men, but as wise, making the most of your time because the days are evil. So then do not be foolish, but understand what the will of the Lord is."

3. *Do not be governed by every emergency.* Set your priorities and goals. Constantly evaluate to make sure you are on track. As Matthew 6:33 recommends, "But seek first his kingdom and his righteousness, and all these things will be given to you as well."Seek ye first the Kingdom of God, then all these things shall be added unto you."

4. *Determine when certain tasks should be performed based on when you are at your best.* Some tasks are better performed at certain times and under certain conditions. For instance, I'm better when I spend the early morning for my quiet times. I'm better at reading books in the summer when the job pressures ease off. We should all know our rhythms and be in touch with how to maximize our time under the appropriate conditions. Ecclesiastes 3:1-11 tells us there is a time for "everything under heaven."

5. *Learn to say "no" to good things, so you can say "yes" to the best.* Psalm 130:5 confesses, "I wait for the Lord, my soul waits, and in His word I put my do I hope."

6. *Budget time far in advance (even months ahead).* Put into your schedule all the non-negotiables such as work responsi-

bilities. Then identify days of rest, personal time with immediate and extended family, date nights, play days...even your quiet time. After these are scheduled then you can drop other items into your schedule. Psalm 31:14-15a stresses, "But I trust in you, O Lord; I say, "You are my God." My times are in your hands..."

7. *Make a list of all unfinished projects, and attempt to do the most difficult one first.* When your list is made, it gives you perspective. Do not put off something that can be done now. It works even better if you can make it your goal to never pick up something twice. Another helpful hint is to make sure everything you have finds a home. If you can't find a place for something, perhaps it is something you shouldn't keep. Organize everything into four piles: To Do, To Pay, To File and To Read. Then when the daily deluge of paper starts, you can find an appropriate place for everything. You'll always know where things are, and you can stop spending your valuable time looking all over the house for that bill you need to pay. Proverbs 14:23 says, "All hard work brings a profit, In all labor there is profit, but mere talk leads only to poverty."

8. *Use a daytimer or calendar that works for you.* Carry it with you, and maintain a simple, useable system. If you are married, review what is on your schedule on a regular basis with your spouse.

9. *Do an accounting of your current daily routine through monitoring time by half-hour increments.* How do you currently spend your time? Through this exercise you will find out what things are chewing up major blocks of time. Specifically, I encourage you to drastically cut down on your TV viewing. This one alone can steal valuable time. Count the hours you and your family spend with the tube. You may be able to find major amounts of time buried there.

HAVE YOU HEARD OF THE 7 HABITS?

One of the most poignant books of our time is Stephen Covey's *The 7 Habits of Highly Effective People* (Simon & Schuster; 1990). (Though not a "Christian book," it contains many insightful, helpful principles). Here are the 7 Habits:

1. **Be Proactive.** Take responsibility for your own effectiveness, happiness and circumstances.

2. **Begin with the End in Mind.** Identify your various roles, then think about the long-term goals you want to accomplish in each of those roles.

3. **Put First Things First.** Having identified roles and goals, now schedule and adapt as necessary to accomplish your goals and "the end" (Habit 2).

4. **Think Win/Win.** Constantly seek mutual benefit in all human interactions.

5. **Seek First to Understand, Then to Be Understood.** Listen to get inside the other person's frame of reference, then present your own ideas contextually.

6. **Synergize.** As "the whole is greater than the sum of its parts," so a group working together can accomplish more than an individual.

7. **Sharpen the Saw.** This focuses on personal renewal. In short, attend to your personal physical, mental, social/emotional and spiritual needs.

[1] Charles E. Hummel, *Tyranny of the Urgent* (Downers Grove, IL: Inter-Varsity Christian Fellowship, 1994 revised).

13

Half Truths and Outright Lies

Have you told any half truths or outright lies, putting yourself in a better light to those around you?

This was a late addition to our list of weekly questions because we realized how many times we tend to be dishonest. Often half truths are spoken out of convenience rather than taking the needed time to be absolutely honest. The irony of a half truth is that it is actually a 100% lie. That is what we try to address and eliminate as part of our regular conversations with others.

"Be more concerned with your character than your reputation because your character is what you really are, while your reputation is merely what others think you are," states John Wooden, former UCLA Head Basketball Coach.[1] I have known people whose character is questioned because their reputation has scarred them. Both their words and actions are not trusted. What a terrible predicament it is when your character is in jeopardy.

It has been said there are three kinds of people: those who say they are great, those who say they are not and those who forget who they are. The first two are subject to pride—one openly, the other through false humility. The last is the person whose eyes are so fixed on Jesus Christ he finds no reason to exalt any other than Him (Ephesians 2:8-10).

WHAT DOES SCRIPTURE SAY?

"Do your best to present yourself to God as one approved, a workman who does not need to be ashamed and who correctly handles the word of truth. Avoid godless chatter, because those who indulge in it will become more and more ungodly." (2 Timothy 2:15-16)

"Likewise the tongue is a small part of the body, but it makes great boasts. Consider what a great forest is set on fire by a small spark. The tongue also is a fire, a world of evil among the parts of the body. It corrupts the whole person, sets the whole course of his life on fire, and is itself set on fire by hell...but no man can tame the tongue. It is a restless evil, full of deadly poison." (James 3:5,6,8)

"The Lord does not look at the things man looks at. Man looks at the outward appearance, but the Lord looks at the heart." (1 Samuel 16:7b)

"But I tell you that men will have to give an account on the day of judgment for every careless word they have spoken. For by your words you will be acquitted, and by your words you will be condemned." (Matthew 12:36-37)

"For whoever exalts himself will be humbled, and whoever humbles himself will be exalted." (Matthew 23:12)

HOW ABOUT A LITTLE HUMILITY?

It is also evident how often we share words to exalt ourselves in the eyes of others. 1 Peter 5:6 says, "Humble yourselves, therefore, under God's mighty hand, that he may lift you up in due time." James 4:6b adds, "God opposes the proud but gives grace to the humble." Why is it so easy to stretch our stories to a point where they become untruth?

It was recently reported that a prominent Christian comedian had been living a lie about his past. When discovered, it sent shock waves through the Christian circles. People were dismayed by discovering the truth behind this person's ministry. He had exaggerated his past by stretching the truth. He said, "I feel that, in some cases, I have stepped over the line between honest ministry and good entertainment. I was not trying to lie. I just wanted to be good at my job, and I forgot to be entirely true to my calling." This has led to an investigation by the IRS into the organization's tax-exempt status as well as put on hold all ministry efforts in a determination to find out the truth.[2]

I believe that most of us do not deliberately seek to lie. Yet it can be very easy to stretch the truth, and this is lying. Many of the guys in our group have been challenged by this question during their conversations on a day-to-day basis. Several have said that they have been in the midst of a half truth and have retracted words right on the spot to make it truthful. More than once, we have all had to swallow our ego and pride and admit to this having been a part of our week.

This issue boils down to integrity. It is complicated when you begin to carry on a lie. Soon you can not keep straight who even knows the truth. Further, a lie shared over and over can eventually start to sound like the truth. It is so much easier to just tell the truth.

Several years ago I met a man who claimed to be a baseball star. After watching him play, I suspected something was not quite right but just thought that perhaps his skills had deteriorated quickly. Yet he persisted in telling me and others about his collegiate and professional background. One day I telephoned the sports information department at his university to find out about his career. As I suspected, he had never played at all. When I confronted him with the truth, it stung him deeply and he ran from me for years. Later I became aware that this was only one incident in a series of self-promoting lies. In his case I believe he became so convinced of the lies that eventually they began to sound to him like the truth. His is a sad story.

Seeking Forgiveness

When you become aware or convicted of a half truth or outright lie, you need to quickly confess your sin to God and man, seek forgiveness and reconcile with those you've lied to and perhaps hurt and offended. Several times in the past few years I have had to plead for forgiveness with a number of people including my wife. Here is a simple forgiveness process involving parties.

The one who offended or lied must: (1) admit he has done something wrong before God and man and (2) then he must specifically, sincerely ask God and the person they offended or hurt for forgiveness.

The one who has been offended must: (1) specifically forgive the person involved and (2) then should do everything possible to not only forgive but to forget the incident. Though this is difficult, to say you are forgiven and then to bring it up and re-hash it again and again is not forgiveness at all.

Living a Life of Integrity

Integrity by definition is "a strict adherence to a moral set of values." This includes utter sincerity, honesty, candor, not artificial, not shallow and no empty promises. Those with integrity are committed to the absolute, unchanging directives as stated in the Bible. God is our model.

Every day we're influenced by the philosophy and values of those around us. In a famous experiment some students put a frog in a container of water and began to heat the water slowly. The water finally reached the boiling point, yet the frog never attempted to jump out. Why? Because the changes in the environment were so subtle that the frog didn't notice them until it was too late.

As Christian men and women, it's easier than we think to end up like the frog. Many godly people—pastors, seminary professors, respected and beloved Christian leaders—have yielded to the world's value system because they failed to discern the subtle changes occurring around and to them. Before they knew it, they were in hot water. They didn't want that. They didn't intend to get there. They didn't think it could happen to them. But it did.

The Bible says "For he chose us in him before the creation of the world to be holy and blameless in his sight" (Ephesians 1:4), to "live a life worthy of the calling you have received" (Ephesians 4:1), to be "mature" (Ephesians 4:13) and "imitators of God" (Ephesians 5:1). When we hear the word "holy," we often think of someone else, not ourselves. The word "holy" refers to something or someone separated and set apart for God. That can include all believers in Christ Jesus.

Here are seven ways that God can help you move beyond good intentions and down the path of integrity:

1. *Make a decision.* In the Old Testament, Daniel chose not to compromise and defile himself. Almost every day you come to some kind of fork in the road. Like Daniel you will face tough choices. What you decide at that fork is greatly influenced by the choices you made earlier.
2. *Choose to put first things first.* Truth must be planted in our hearts daily. It isn't merely reading but allowing the Holy Spirit to plant the truths of Scripture deep into our hearts and minds through consistent Bible reading and memorization, meditation and prayer.
3. *Determine where the line is, and then stay a safe distance behind it.* Determine what kinds of things are healthy and unhealthy. Whatever distracts or weakens us will put us at risk. Determine where the line is and if it's not something that is clear in Scripture, then pray about it and seek the

counsel of several wise friends. Once you've decided where the line is, walk ten yards back, and make that your line! Always leave yourself a margin.

4. *Guard your heart.* We can't serve two masters (Matthew 6:21).

5. *Guard your mind.* The mind is the place where decisions are made for or against the truth. What we choose to read, watch and think about will determine, to a great degree, whether we will be victims or victors, conquered or conquerors.

6. *Guard your eyes.* Joseph was smart (Genesis 39), and Job knew the importance of guarding his eyes (Job 31:1), but David lingered too long, stared a bit too much and unwisely entertained unhealthy fantasy. He didn't guard his eyes and ended up committing adultery with Bathsheba and murdered her husband.

7. *Guard the little things.* Luke 16:10 says, "Whoever can be trusted with very little can also be trusted with much." How we handle the seemingly little things determines, over time, our response to big things. Be on guard against rationalization, little lies, itsy bitsy temptations and trying to justify your actions.[3]

The Seven Promises of a Promise Keeper

Author's Note: The growth of the Promise Keeper's organization has been one of the most phenomenal ever witnessed. Founded in 1990 by former Colorado University's head football coach Bill McCartney, the initial goal was to fill C.U.'s Folsom Field with 50,000 men gathered to honor Jesus Christ and to learn more about becoming godly men. In three short years this goal was realized at Promise Keeper's '93. In 1994 almost 250,000 men attended six conferences held across America.

Their purpose statement is "Promise Keepers is a Christ-centered ministry dedicated to uniting men through vital relationships to become godly influences in their world." They are seeking men who understand that becoming a Promise Keeper is a process and who acknowledge the grace and strength available through Jesus Christ in this process. They have identified seven areas of a man's life which are directly affected by this commitment.

1. A Promise Keeper is committed to honor Jesus Christ through worship, prayer and obedience to His word.
2. A Promise Keeper is committed to practice spiritual, moral, ethical and sexual purity.
3. A Promise Keeper is committed to build strong marriages and families through love, protection and Biblical values.
4. A Promise Keeper is committed to support the mission of his church by honoring and praying for his pastor and by actively giving his time and resources.
5. A Promise Keeper is committed to reach beyond any racial and denominational barriers to demonstrate the power of Biblical unity.
6. A Promise Keeper is committed to influence His world, being obedient to the Great Commandment (Mark 12:30-31) and the Great Commission (Matthew 28:19-20).
7. A Promise Keeper is committed to pursue vital relationships with a few other men, understanding that he needs brothers to help him keep his promises.

To find out more about the Promise Keeper's organization in your area contact them at P.O. Box 18376, Boulder, CO 80308. Phone: 303-421-2800 or FAX: 303-421-2918.

[1] Coach Wooden shared this quote while attending the 1992 FCA Camp at Thousand Oaks, California.
[2] Contemporary Christian Music magazine, May 1993, p. 28.
[3] Dr. Gary Oliver, Adapted from *Seven Promises of a Promise Keeper* (Colorado Springs, CO: Focus on the Family, 1994), pp. 84-90.

14

Sharing The Gospel

Have you shared the Gospel with an unbeliever this week?

God could have planned from the very beginning of time to use anything to tell the world about Him. For some reason He chose the human race. While on this earth we have a responsibility to share the truths of God, His Son Jesus Christ and the plan of salvation with the people who are placed in our lives. It is important to remember that the Holy Spirit is the one who convicts and changes the heart of an unbeliever. We are not called to coerce people into accepting Christ. We are called to be used by God as He sees fit to help bring people to the point of making a decision to accept or reject Christ.

Regardless of how bold you may be, we are all called to live out Matthew 5:13-16: "You are the salt of the earth. But if the salt loses its saltiness, how can it be made salty again? It is no longer good for anything, except to be thrown out and trampled by men. You are the light of the world. A city on the hill cannot be hidden. Neither do people light a lamp and put it under a bowl. Instead they put it on its stand, and it gives light to everyone in the house. In the same way, let your light shine before men, that they may see your good deeds and praise your Father in heaven." By its nature, salt prevents corruption in the preservation of goods. It creates taste and it improves taste. By its nature, light illuminates and shows the way through darkness.

Dr. Glenn Wagner, shared at the Promise Keeper's 1993 Leadership Conference, "You could easily define the meaning of the world as relationships and even these fit a 10/10/80 principle: 10% will change if you give them good information; 10% will never change no matter what information you give them; 80% will change if a relationship is involved."

What Does Scripture Say?

"The goal of this command is love, which comes from a pure heart and a good conscience and a sincere faith." (1 Timothy 1:5)

"But in your hearts set apart Christ as Lord. Always be prepared to give an answer to everyone who asks you to give the reason for the hope you have. But do this with gentleness and respect." (1 Peter 3:15)

"For God did not give us a spirit of timidity, but a spirit of power, of love and of self-discipline. So do not be ashamed to testify about our Lord,..."(2 Timothy 1:7-8)

"No one who denies the Son has the Father; whoever acknowledges the Son has the Father also." (1 John 2:23)

"Whoever acknowledges me before men, I will also acknowledge him before my Father in heaven. But whoever disowns me before men, I will disown him before my Father in heaven." (Matthew 10:32-33)

People Are Watching

Those who watch you closely or from afar should be able to see the light and taste the salt that pours out from you. Don't be surprised by how closely people are watching you. As the song says, "You're the only Jesus that some people may ever see." I Peter 2:12 says it this way, "Live such good lives among the pagans that, though they accuse you of doing wrong, they may see your good deeds and glorify God on the day he visits us."

In Matthew 13:1-23, we see the parable of the Sower and the Four Soils. All of us have a responsibility to plant seeds of faith to a watching world. Others are called to water the seeds and eventually collect the harvest. Only God can take credit for the final acceptance, yet we play an important role in living out and communicating our faith with others.

I believe the first step in presenting the gospel to someone is by initiating and establishing a relationship. If within that relationship you get an opportunity to share the gospel, then that is wonderful. In addition to forging a friendship, keep your eyes and ears open to sharing what God has done in your life. Perhaps you will have fertile soil with an opportunity to plunge right in to the gospel. In other cases there may be a long season of planting seeds awaiting the right moment to share your faith. There may not be a perfect time to witness. Yet as a relationship is developed, ask God to give you a natural opportunity.

I will admit that I get nervous and a bit tongue-tied when I try to articulate my faith to someone, but what joy there is when someone hears the truth of God and responds by making a decision to follow Him. And because of this reason, I have made 2 Timothy 4:2 my prayer that I would "be prepared in season and out of season." This means that I am always prepared when called upon or prompted by God to testify for Jesus Christ and His wonderful work within me. Are you ready at a moment's notice to tell someone your story of coming to a faith in Christ? If not, I challenge you today to work on a 3-5 minute testimony which during that time you can tell what you were like before receiving Christ, how you met Christ and what He has done to change your life since accepting Him.

Obviously, I do not get the opportunity to witness every single day, but I am ready. Also, I would not get hung up on feeling like you need to know every single theological argument and biblical reference before you communicate your faith. I love the story of the blind man in John 9. When questioned by the authorities, the blind man did not know all the answers, but one thing he did know from verse 25, "I was blind but now I see!" In simple terms his life was changed, and he was telling people about it.

Telling the good news of Christ is an incredible experience. You do not need to look far to find people who need Christ. This includes family members, neighbors, co-workers and others you may meet in the course of day-to-day life. In many ways the most difficult prospects may be family members because they know us the best.

Several in our accountability group get many opportunities to present their faith to others. As the Kansas City Chiefs mascot, Dan Meers gets multiple opportunities on a daily basis to testify to thousands of young people through school assembly programs. Mike DeBacker, within his engineering firm, is not shy about spreading his enthusiasm for Christ with those he works with. My wife Janna has many chances to share her faith with fellow nurses and patients. Several years ago, I got the chance to play softball on a team of non-Christians, and it was a wonderful opportunity to let the Lord use me to be "salt and light" in that environment. We have found that so many are eager to know God and are responsive to us to find out why we are different.

Even in interacting with people who may only cross your path for a few minutes, you still have a chance to live out God's love before them. In these cases I encourage you to keep your antenna up and listen for opportunities where you can live out the good news. Regardless of what you say or the time you will get to do so, let your light shine.

A Three Legged Stool

John 15 shows that Jesus gave instructions on three key relationships: With Jesus, with fellow believers and with the world. Do you have these three key relationships? Are all three being handled properly? If a 3-legged stool is missing one leg, it isn't complete and therefore it topples over. How would your rate if these relationships were each a leg on a 3-legged stool?

Some people have a great relationship with God, but they can't get along with Christians, or they easily slip back in the ways of the world from time to time. Others have great relationships with believers but hardly spend any time (if at all) with God, or the pressures of the world pulls them down. Some enjoy the world so much that no one even knows that they are a Christian.

To maximize each of these relationships, first develop your walk with Christ, and then ask Him to give you a heart to positively interact with the believers and the world. And while we are in the world, do not get seduced by its temptations, but instead be a witness for Christ. We are called to go into the world and woo people for Christ in our community. It is not just an inviting them to church but giving them your time.

EVERYONE IS A HIGH PRIEST

When I was a member at University Presbyterian Church in Seattle, their motto was "every member a high priest." It communicated a message that every person in the congregation played an important part in the kingdom of God, in touching and serving the needs of others. Hebrews 5:1-3 tells us, "Every high priest is selected from among men and is appointed to represent them in matters related to God, to offer gifts and sacrifices for sins. He is able to deal gently with those who are ignorant and are going astray, since he himself is subject to weakness. This is why he has to offer sacrifices for his own sins, as well as for the sins of the people." These scriptures point out so well that the high priest was a weak person yet played an important part in reaching and touching others.

After all, the only perfect high priest was Jesus Christ. Hebrews 7:26-28 says, "Such a high priest meets our need—one who is holy, blameless, pure, set apart from sinners, exalted above the heavens. Unlike the other high priests, he does not need to offer sacrifices day after day, first for his own sins, and then for the sins of the people. He sacrificed for their sins once for all when he offered himself. For the law appoints as high priests men who are weak; but the oath, which came after the law, appointed the Son, who has been made perfect forever."

Keys To Sharing Your Testimony

The purpose of a testimony is to introduce others to Jesus Christ. Your audience may be in a one-on-one setting or a large group of people. The goal, through the power of the Holy Spirit, is to move people either toward the point of conversion at the cross or beyond the cross into maturing obedience in Christ. Regardless of the opportunity be ready to give an accurate account, and clearly communicate who Jesus Christ is in your life.

An outline for building your testimony should include:

1. How you came to know Christ personally.
2. Identify the specific steps of salvation including: Recognition of the need for Christ in your life, turning away from the sinfulness of your life, accepting Christ's forgiveness for your sin and receiving Jesus Christ as Savior and Lord.
3. Scripture is crucial to illustrate and document what has happened.

4. Cover the basics of the gospel including: Man's sinfulness which separates us from God; the life, teachings, death and resurrection of Jesus Christ as the payment (atonement) for man's sins; and through faith in Jesus we are redeemed into "new life" as outlined in 1 Corinthians 15:1-4.
5. Your new life in Christ. Speak of the changes Christ has brought in your life and what He means to you. Talk about things that will cause others to want to know Him as well. (*Note:* Be real...not pie in the sky. Include challenging and specific times of growth).
6. In your conclusion use an illustration (if appropriate) to capture the theme of your testimony.
7. Tell how they can become a Christian by reviewing the meaning of salvation, presenting Scripture and if appropriate, be ready to issue a call to commitment.
8. Close in prayer.

If you can do all of the above in less than five minutes, it is ideal. Obviously, if you have more time, you can expand. By having the basics down to five minutes, you can quickly determine what is the most important aspects, and remove the extraneous thoughts. Determine the time frame you have before you start. Use wisdom in selecting Scripture references. Too many or too few can work against you.

Be conscious of not using religious terminology, cliches or phrases which the unchurched may not be familiar or cause them to be uncomfortable. Also, be careful with particular denominational dogmas or doctrines which could sidetrack the overall purpose. Negative comments about people, churches, denominations or issues can be counter productive.

The World's Bible

Christ has no hands but our hands to do His work today;
He has no feet but our feet to lead men in His way;
He has no tongues but our tongues to tell men how He died;
He has no help but our help to bring them to His side.
We are the only Bible the careless world will read;
We are the sinner's gospel; we are the scoffer's creed;
We are the Lord's last message given in death and work.
What if the line is crooked? What if the type is blurred?
What if our hands are busy with other work than His?
What if our feet are walking where sin's allurement is?
What if our tongues are speaking of things His lips would spurn?
How can we hope to help Him unless from Him we learn?

Author Unknown

15

Exercise, Eating and Sleeping

Have you taken care of your body through daily physical exercise and proper eating and sleeping habits?

All three of these areas represent my favorite activities, yet they also get greatly abused and neglected. When these areas are in good working order, I feel fresh and confident, ready to take on any challenge. When abused and neglected, I am lethargic and frustrated.

WHAT DOES SCRIPTURE SAY?

The body God has given us is our only shot. Therefore, we need to treat it properly. 1 Corinthians 6:19-20 warns, "Do you not know that your body is a temple of the Holy Spirit, who is in you, whom you have received from God? You are not your own; you were bought at a price. Therefore honor God with your body."

Psalms 139 talks about how intricately we were made and developed in the womb. Developed from 21 chromosomes from each parent, we become one specially created person. We have 206 bones, muscles, joints, ligaments and tendons making up an active body. We have a responsibility to care properly for what God has created.

Physical Exercise

Not only do I feel much better when I am on a regular workout schedule, but I also believe it enhances all the other areas of my life including improved productivity, creative energy, greater concentration and better relationships. Depending on your age and previous exercise history, you may want to get a check-up before embarking on a new exercise program.

If possible, I encourage you to have three workout days scheduled as part of your week. It can range from a hard ten mile run or a racquetball game to a walk through the neighborhood. Bicycling, aerobics, weight lifting programs, basketball, golfing (carry your clubs), softball, etc. are options available to you.

Conditioning Programs: The key is doing something which will elevate your heart rate to 60% to 85% of your maximum heart rate (see chart below), and sustaining it for an appropriate time period (normally 20 to 60 minutes). Situps and pushups every morning or evening in your home are excellent.

Exercise increases your body's need for oxygen. In order to deliver more oxygen to working muscles, your heart must work harder to pump blood throughout your body. Continued throughout your life, exercise ultimately makes your heart stronger and decreases your chance of developing heart disease. In addition, regular exercise improves the tone and efficiency of your muscles and enhances your lung function.

Before you start your fitness journey, it is a good idea to know what you want to accomplish. Do you want to lose weight, or are you headed toward cardiorespiratory fitness? Your goal will determine the intensity of your workout.

High intensity exercise for shorter periods of time promotes cardiorespiratory improvement, and burns mostly muscle glycogen as fuel. This helps reduce the possibility of heart disease and improves endurance. A low-intensity workout for longer periods of time burns more calories from stored fat.

Regardless of your fitness goals, remember to warm up and cool down by stretching for at least 15 minutes before and after you exercise, using gradual, non-bouncing movements. You'll increase your muscle elasticity and help decrease the chance of muscular strain. A proper cool down period helps remove the end products of exercise, including lactic acid. Your body will thank you by not being so sore.

CHART GUIDE FOR MAXIMUM HEART RATE

Exercising too hard or not hard enough can be ineffective. For best results, determine your maximum heart rate range by subtracting your age from 220:

**220-(your age) = (maximum heart rate)

If your goal is FAT LOSS, use the following formula to determine your training zone:

**(maximum heart rate) x 60%= Lower limit

**(maximum heart rate) x 75% = Upper limit

If your goal is CARDIORESPIRATORY FITNESS, your effective training zone will be higher. Use the following formula to determine your training zone:

**(maximum heart rate) x 75% = Lower limit

**(maximum heart rate) x 85% = Upper limit

EXAMPLE: Age 35 (220-35 = 185)

FAT LOSS TRAINING:

185 x .60 = 111 beats/min. (lower limit)

185 x .75 = 139 beats/min. (upper limit)

CARDIORESPIRATORY TRAINING:
185 x .75 = 139 beats/min. (lower limit)
185 x .85 = 157 beats/min. (upper limit)

Strength Training: In strength training you increase your muscle strength (your ability to lift heavy objects) and muscular endurance (your ability to repeat a movement requiring strength). Regular strength training can help build strength, power and endurance, control weight, lower body fat, improve appearance and build self-confidence. It helps lower the risk of injury to muscles, ligaments and tendons. Properly conditioned muscles are also essential to carry out the activities of your daily life and vital to a safer performance in sports and aerobic conditioning programs. A well-rounded fitness program will include both strength and endurance programs.

Keys before you lift include: start at a comfortable level, warm up properly, learn the proper lifting techniques, exercise major muscle groups, exercise large muscles first (chest, back and abdomen prior to biceps, triceps and smaller muscle groups), alternate muscle groups to reduce risk injury, challenge yourself by increasing weight and resistance over time, and give yourself at least a day of rest between workouts.

Proper Eating

Weight loss has been one of the major issues we have discussed within our group because it is a battle we all face. Though not a nutritionist, I have learned that fat grams are like the kiss of death to any weight loss. Unfortunately, everything I enjoy consuming is loaded with fat grams. Janna has helped me be more conscious of the things I eat, and my accountability group has helped keep me focused on my goals.

Instead of counting calories, pay attention to where they come from. Calories from carbohydrates are less likely to be stored as fat and more likely to energize muscles than calories from fat. Ideally your diet should be made up of 55-60% carbohydrates, 10-15% protein and less than 30% fat. High carbohydrate foods include bread, cereal, pasta, crackers and rice. Fats, oils and sweets should be avoided, while reasonable levels of vegetables, fruits, milk products and meat/poultry/fish should be included as part of your nutrition.

SLEEPING HABITS

Don't snicker...this one is also important. One of the keys to my entire day is how well and how much sleep I got the night before. I would love to get a solid, eight hours a day. Unfortunately, my love for the late night makes this almost an impossibility. Janna has helped me to be aware of this area.

Here are some keys to success for these three areas (exercise, eating and sleeping):

1. Begin. "I'll start tomorrow" does not work. It is important to identify your need, and begin today. Set aside time to properly stretch, and begin a regular walking/jogging program as part of your daily schedule. Exercise experts say physical activity by itself makes us leaner and healthier, sleep more deeply and shrug off stress.
2. Look for daily activity. Some type of activity seems to help suppress appetites. "The exercising body knows what it should eat, when to sleep, why it shouldn't smoke and how much alcohol to drink," says Dwight Gaal, an exercise physiologist who designs fitness programs for the UAW, Ford Motor Co. and other employers. "I firmly believe, once somebody finds exercise and adopts it, then everything else falls into place," Gaal says.

3. Work briskly. Try to complete your activity within 45 minutes. Include some resistance exercise like lifting weights as part of your workout.
4. Diets don't always work, but low fat nutrition can. Once you start to exercise, you will increase weight loss by trimming fat from your diet.
5. Participate in activities you enjoy, and get friends to join you.
6. Record your progress. Keep a log, and develop a reward system for outstanding efforts and accomplishments. Tell others. Going public with a goal helps you stay with it.
7. Think long-term. Exercise, eating right and getting the right amount of sleep can't just be a one month deal. Shoot for the long-term. Be realistic in your goal-setting.

Alcohol, Smoking and Illegal Drugs

Fortunately, our group does not have people who are battling addictions to alcohol, smoking or illegal drugs, so little if any time has been dedicated to these subjects. If anyone in your group needs help in any of these areas, develop accountability questions where you can help those in need.

There are guidelines that each of us should consider when faced with these temptations:

1. When prohibited by law, do not use. If you are under age, in a county where it is illegal, or if it is a crime, this is a no-brainer. Don't do it!
2. Consider others. Something may not seem wrong to you, but it may cause a serious "stumbling block" to someone else. Consider the following Scriptures:

"And if anyone causes one of these little ones who believe in me to sin, it would be better for him to be thrown into the sea with a large millstone tied around his neck." (Mark 9:42)

"So I strive always to keep my conscience clear before God and man." (Acts 24:16)

"So then, each of us will give an account of himself to God. Therefore let us stop passing judgment on one another. Instead, make up your mind not to put any stumbling block or obstacle in your brother's way." (Romans 14:12-13)

"Everything is permissible"—but not everything is beneficial. "Everything is permissible"—but not everything is constructive. Nobody should seek his own good, but the good of others." (1 Corinthians 10:23-24)

3. *Be careful and honest with yourself.* I have known people who have innocently begun using the above and either become addicted and/or greatly influenced to the point where it changes them (temporarily or permanently). This is particularly true of alcohol use. Personally, I see little reason to have any of these in the life of a Christian. Abstinence really makes things much simpler, and it opens up lots of opportunities to tell others about Christ.

EIGHT POINTS TO LIVING A CONSISTENT CHRISTIAN WALK

by Harold Reynolds, Major League Baseball Player

Author's Note: I heard Harold give this talk at an FCA event. "Vision" can be defined as something (or anything) that you want to accomplish.

1. *Have a vision.* Habakkuk 2:2 says to write your vision down, so you'll recognize it when it unfolds. We have to know our reason for living.
2. *Commit to the vision.* Just like focusing a camera, making a commitment focuses our vision, making it clearer and clearer to us. It helps to begin with the end in mind which will allow you to see the outcome before others see it.
3. *Don't get distracted or discouraged from the vision.* Jesus came so we could have life, but Satan wants to kill and to destroy.

4. *Stay on the right path because it builds confidence.* Proverbs 4:18 says, "The path of the righteous is like the first gleam of dawn, shining ever brighter till the full light of day." The further you go along, the clearer things will get.

5. *Allow the vision to mature.* Sometimes we give up too fast—like marriages where everything is great during the initial months, but the couple divorces within a year. It takes nine months for a baby to develop and mature within the womb before it is born. As Christians, we need to have patience in our spiritual growth. Growth takes time. We should remember this when we bring people to Christ. We must provide for follow-up, not just say, "I'm glad you've made a commitment. Now grow up."

6. *Develop good work habits.* Excellence in any area of life demands good work habits...whether it's prayer, Bible reading or baseball. I've worked on my swing and developed good habits in baseball, and even though I'll still have rough times, those good baseball habits will get me through.

7. *Run through the tape.* You've all seen sprinters lean into the tape at the end of the race. In the spiritual race of life it's not how well you start but who endures to the end and leans to the tape (1 Corinthians 9:24-25).

8. *Remember the vision because the vision keeps you alive.* Proverbs 29:18 reminds us that when there is no vision, we perish.

Author's Note: Much of the information pertaining to exercise was supplied by Kathy Cosgrove, who is a exercise physiologist/personal trainer in the Kansas City area.

16

Joy and Happiness

Have you allowed any person or circumstance to rob you of your joy?

This question was recommended to me by FCA's, Van Normand and helped complete our question series. There is a distinct difference between joy and happiness. Joy is described as "feeling contentment and peace inside because God's in charge outside." Joy isn't based on emotional feelings or events. It is a deep, ongoing certainty and peace that no matter how rotten life is, God's still in control and with you through every situation. Though your self-image may take a beating, real joy is knowing God loves you deeply and unconditionally.

Happiness is often based on external circumstances or temporary situations. For instance, if the weather is lousy or a friend is rude, it can ruin our day. In our daily routine are there incidents where we allow people or circumstances to rob us of our joy? This could range from frustrations in driving in slow traffic, having a flooded basement, working with a difficult employee or a variety of other things.

How you react to these difficult situations can have a tremendous effect on not only your own spirit but also on the attitudes of those close to you.

Author Paul Sailhammer says, "Joy is that deep settled confidence that God is in control of every area of my life." Tim Hansel believes, "Joy is not a feeling; it is a choice. It is not based upon circumstances; it is based upon attitude. It is free, but it is not cheap. It is the by-product of a growing relationship with Jesus Christ. It is a promise, not a deal. It is available to us when we make ourselves available to him. It is something that we can receive by invitation and by choice. It requires commitment, courage and endurance." He also states, "Pain is inevitable, but misery is optional. We cannot avoid pain, but we can avoid joy. God has given us such immense freedom that He will allow us to be as miserable as we want to be." John McArthur points out, "There is no event or circumstance that can occur in the life of any Christian that should diminish that Christian's joy."[1]

There is no question that the day-to-day grind of life is difficult. John 16:33 Jesus reminds us that in the world we will experience trouble. There will be tribulation, but we are not merely to endure it but to "be of good cheer" for He has overcome the world.

Being "successful" doesn't necessarily mean you will experience joy. Many in the world have achieved riches, power, fame and popularity, yet are miserable. They have attained their success but have paid the high costs of losing family, friends and even their own soul. Steve Largent, future NFL Hall of Famer, warns about climbing the ladder of success but at the top rung discovering that the ladder had been leaning against the wrong structure. How tragic when people make this discovery.

True success is walking in obedience with God, meditating on His Word, day and night (Joshua 1:7-8). And as Dal Shealy, FCA National President, admonishes, "It's your attitude, not your aptitude, that allows you to get to a higher altitude, if you have enough intestinal fortitude."

WHAT DOES SCRIPTURE SAY?

"Therefore, since we are surrounded by such a great cloud of witnesses, let us throw off everything that hinders and the sin that so easily entangles, and let us run with perseverance the race marked out for us. Let us fix our eyes on Jesus, the author and perfecter of our faith, who for the joy set before him endured the cross, scorning its shame, and sat down at the right hand of the throne of God. Consider him who endured such opposition from sinful men, so that you will not grow weary and lose heart." (Hebrews 12:1-3)

THE OBJECT OF OUR SEARCH

In the 17th century, a French monk, Father Marin Mersenne, discovered a prime number which could be used to calculate a perfect number. For those of us who are not mathematically inclined, a prime number is one that can be divided only by one, or itself, and a perfect number is one that's the sum of all its factors.

Ever since that time mathematicians have been looking for more "Mersenne primes." Recently, the 32nd such number was discovered by David Slowinski, using a super-computer. It fills 32 computer pages and contains 455,633 digits.

But Slowinski would be the first to admit, his discovery really can't be used for anything. He was quoted as saying, "We couldn't look at it and discover anything. Not that I know of." Mathematicians, throughout the world, will be excited about his discovery, but excepting for the publicity, it will be of no practical value.

Many of us go through life searching for things which are really meaningless—especially in the spiritual realm. We seek meaning to life, without ever including God in our search. It is only through Him, we can have abundant life (John 10:10). We seek security in material things which will soon decay, and forget to "store up for yourselves treasures on earth, where moth and rust do not destroy" (Matthew 6:20). We seek happiness in the pleasures of this world and forget the source of true happiness. The Psalmist said, "You have made known to me the path of life; you will fill me with joy in your presence, with eternal pleasures at your right hand." (Psalm 16:11)

All of us go through life seeking something. Some of us will come to the end of our lives, and have to admit our search has turned up nothing of lasting, eternal value. Others, however, will follow Psalm 105:4, "Look to the Lord and his strength; seek his face always." He can make a difference in our lives, both now, and throughout eternity.[2]

Overcoming Obstacles

The following poem depicts the attitude we need as we meet various obstacles in life.

The Race

"Quit! Give up, you're beaten," they shout and plead,
"There's just too much against you now. This time you can't succeed."
And as I start to hang my head in front of failure's face,
My downward fall is broken by the memory of a race.
And hope refills my weakened will as I recall that scene,
For just the thought of that short race rejuvenates my being.
A children's race, young boys, young men; how I remember well,
Excitement sure, but also fear, it wasn't hard to tell.
They all lined up so full of hope. Each thought to win that race,
Or tie for first, or if not that, at least take second place.
And fathers watched from off the side, each cheering for his son,
And each boy hoped to show his dad that he would be the one.

The whistle blew, and off they went, young hearts and hopes of fire.
To win, to be the hero there, was each young boy's desire.
And one boy in particular, his dad was in the crowd,

Was running near the lead and thought, "My dad will be so proud."
But as he speeded down the field across a shallow dip,
The little boy who thought to win, lost his step and slipped.
Trying hard to catch himself, his hands flew out to brace,
And mid the laughter of the crowd, he fell flat on his face.
So down he fell and with him hope. He couldn't win it now.
Embarrassed, sad, he only wished to disappear somehow.
But, as he fell, his dad stood up and showed his anxious face,
Which to the boy so clearly said, "Get up and win that race!"

He quickly rose, no damage done, behind a bit that's all,
And ran with all his mind and might to make up for his fall.
So anxious to restore himself, to catch up and to win,
His mind went faster than his legs. He slipped and fell again.
He wished that he had quit before with only one disgrace.
"I'm hopeless as a runner now. I shouldn't try to race."
But in the laughing crowd he searched and found his father's face,
That steady look that said again, "Get up and win that race!"

So he jumped up to try again, ten yards behind the last.
"If I'm to gain those yards," he thought, "I've got to run real fast."
Exceeding everything he had, he regained eight or ten,
But trying so hard to catch the lead, he slipped and fell again.
Defeat!! He lay there silently, a tear dropped from his eye.
"There's no sense running anymore—three strikes, I'm out—why try?"
The will to rise had disappeared, all hope had fled away,
So far behind, so error prone, closer all the way.
"I've lost, so what's the use," he thought, "I'll live with my disgrace."
But then he thought about his dad who soon he'd have to face.
"Get up," an echo sounded low, "Get up and take your place.
You were not meant for failure here. Get up and win that race."

With borrowed will, "Get up," it said, "You haven't lost at all,
For winnings not more than this—to rise each time you fall."
So up he rose to win once more, and with a new commit,
He resolved that win or lose, at least he wouldn't quit.
So far behind the others now, the most he'd ever been,
Still he gave it all he had and ran as though to win.
Three times he'd fallen stumbling, three times he rose again,
Too far behind to hope to win, he still ran to the end.

They cheered the winning runner as he crossed, first place,
Head high and proud and happy; no falling, no disgrace.
But when the fallen youngster crossed the line, last place,
The crowd gave him the greater cheer for finishing the race.
And even though he came in last, with head bowed low, unproud;
You would have thought he won the race, to listen to the crowd.
And to his dad he sadly said, "I didn't do so well."
"To me, you won," his father said, "You rose each time you fell."

And now when things seem dark and hard and difficult to face,
The memory of that little boy helps me in my own race.
For all of life is like that race, with ups and downs and all,
And all you have to do to win is rise each time you fall.
"Quit! Give up, you're beaten," they still shout in my face.
But another voice within me says, "Get up and win that race."

Author Unknown

[1] The quotes from Paul Sailhammer, Tim Hansel and John McArthur were made but unidentifiable to their source. Every effort was made to do so.

[2] This section titled, "The Object of Your Search" was printed on the back of a church bulletin. No source was identified.

17

Wrapping It Up

Have you lied to us on any of your answers today?

Each week, we close our time by asking this deliberate question. I can only recall once, where we got down to this question and one of members had to confess that he needed to come clean on a previous answer.

As previously mentioned, accountability helps play a very important part of our Christian growth. I have grown so much over these past few years by being answerable to people on areas of my public, personal and private life. I encourage you to seek out people who share your desire to also be accountable. I pray you would be as blessed as I have been.

No two groups will be identical, because every person brings unique skills and talents, a different background and maturity level. Utilize the concepts and questions of this book, to develop a model which will ultimately bring you closer to Jesus Christ.

Finishing Well
by Bobby Clinton, Fuller Seminary

Biblical studies show only one in three finishing well. Finishing well means different things to different people. The classic Old Testament character who finished well and demonstrated all of the characteristics was Daniel. The classic New Testament character who finished well is Paul. Here are six major characteristics that help me assess a good finish:

1. They maintain a *personal vibrant relationship* with God right up to the end.
2. They maintain a *learning posture* and can learn from various kinds of sources—life especially.
3. They evidence *Christ-likeness in character* (godliness—you like to be around them).
4. Truth is lived out in their lives so that *convictions* and promises of God are seen to be real.
5. They leave behind one or more *ultimate contributions* (saint, stylistic practitioners, mentors, public rhetoricians, pioneers, crusaders, artists, founder, stabilizers, researchers, writers, promoters).
6. They walk with a growing awareness of a *sense of destiny* and see some or all of it fulfilled.